FOREIGN DIRECT INVESTMENT IN THE UNITED STATES

EDWARD M. GRAHAM
PAUL R. KRUGMAN

Foreign Direct Investment in the United States

INSTITUTE FOR INTERNATIONAL ECONOMICS
WASHINGTON, DC 1989

Edward M. Graham, a Visiting Fellow at the Institute, is Associate Professor in the Fuqua School of Business at Duke University. He was formerly Principal Administrator of the Planning and Evaluation Unit of the Organization for Economic Cooperation and Development in Paris and an International Economist in the Office of International Investment Affairs at the US Treasury. He has written extensively in the areas of international corporate strategy and investment.

Paul R. Krugman, a Visiting Fellow at the Institute, is Professor of Economics at the Massachusetts Institute of Technology. He formerly served as Senior International Economist on the staff of the Council of Economic Advisers. He is the editor of *Strategic Trade Policy and the New International Economics* (1986) and the author of *Exchange-Rate Instability* (1989) as well as other books and articles on international trade and monetary economics.

INSTITUTE FOR INTERNATIONAL ECONOMICS
11 Dupont Circle, NW
Washington, DC 20036
(202) 328-9000 Telex: 261271 IIE UR
FAX: (202) 328-5432

C. Fred Bergsten, *Director*
Linda Griffin Kean, *Director of Publications*

The Institute for International Economics was created by, and receives substantial support from, the German Marshall Fund of the United States.

The views expressed in this publication are those of the authors. This publication is part of the overall program of the Institute, as endorsed by its Board of Directors, but does not necessarily reflect the views of individual members of the Board or the Advisory Committee.

Printed in the United States of America
93 92 91 90 89   5 4 3 2 1

Library of Congress Cataloging-in-Publication Data

Graham, Edward M.
(Edward Montgomery), 1944-
  Foreign direct investment in the United States/Edward M. Graham, Paul R. Krugman.
  Includes bibliographical references and index
  1. Investments, Foreign—United States.
I. Krugman, Paul R.   II. Title.
HG4910.G74   1989   89-29485
332.6'73'0973—dc20   CIP

ISBN 0–88132–074–9

Contents

Figures

To our wives,
Mary Graham and Robin Bergman

Preface

The rapid shift in global economic relationships is nowhere more apparent than with respect to foreign direct investment (FDI). Until quite recently, most of the analytical and policy concerns on this issue were focused in two directions: on the flow of FDI from the United States into Canada, Europe, and the developing countries, and on the potential global power of the multinational firms themselves. Books with such titles as *Le Défi Américain*, *Sovereignty at Bay*, and *Global Reach* were widely read and discussed.

In the 1980s, however, the United States has become the world's largest host country to FDI as well as the largest home country of multinationals. By 1988, moreover, inward FDI by foreign-based companies exceeded investment abroad by American-based firms (at least on the official book-value data published by the US Department of Commerce). The rapid rise of Japanese FDI, in particular, opened another front in the debate over US relations with that country. Congress began to address the issue through several hotly debated provisions of the Omnibus Trade and Competitiveness Act of 1988.

This study is the first attempt at a comprehensive analysis of inward FDI since the phenomenon has become so important to the American economy and thus to its international economic policy. It assesses the nature and causes of FDI, its effect on the economy and national security of the United States, and what policy measures—domestic and international—should and should not be adopted in response.

The study was conducted by Edward M. Graham of the Fuqua School of Business at Duke University and Paul R. Krugman of the Massachusetts Institute of Technology. Both authors spent substantial periods as Visiting Fellows at the Institute for International Economics during preparation of the study from early 1988 through the summer of 1989. They were ably assisted by a study group of experts on FDI from the government, the business community, and academia. I would like to add my personal gratitude to that of the authors for the group's assistance.

The Institute for International Economics is a private nonprofit research institution for the study and discussion of international economic policy. Its purpose is to analyze important issues in that area and to develop and communicate practical new approaches for dealing with them. The Institute is completely nonpartisan.

The Institute was created by a generous commitment of funds from the German Marshall Fund of the United States in 1981 and now receives about 15 percent of its support from that source. In addition, major institutional grants are being provided by the Ford Foundation, the William and Flora Hewlett Foundation, and the Alfred P. Sloan Foundation. A number of other foundations and private corporations are contributing to the increasing diversification of the Institute's financial resources. The John M. Olin Foundation provided partial support for this project.

The Board of Directors bears overall responsibility for the Institute and gives general guidance and approval to its research program, including identification of topics that are likely to become important to international economic policymakers over the medium run (generally one to three years) and which thus should be addressed by the Institute. The Director, working closely with the staff and outside Advisory Committee, is responsible for the development of particular projects and makes the final decision to publish an individual study.

The Institute hopes that its studies and other activities will contribute to building a stronger foundation for international economic policy around the world. Comments as to how it can best do so are invited from the readers of these publications.

C. FRED BERGSTEN
Director
October 1989

Acknowledgments

This study reflects the contributions of many hands other than our own, although we of course bear responsibility for all of the study's failings. The members of the IIE study group on foreign direct investment provided crucial guidance. Officials at the Bureau of Economic Analysis were extremely helpful with both data and interpretive suggestions, as were officials elsewhere in the US Department of Commerce, the US Department of the Treasury, and the US Department of Defense.

Richard N. Cooper, Rachel McCulloch, and Raymond Vernon provided detailed reviews of early drafts of the manuscript, which helped us greatly improve the later versions. Ted Moran also provided valuable comments.

We received help from many members of the staff of the Institute for International Economics. Among these, Amelia Porges helped us immensely with legal matters, Michael Treadway provided vital editorial help, and C. Fred Bergsten provided guidance and assistance throughout the process.

Finally, Rose Marie Ham provided extraordinary research assistance.

E.M.G. and P.R.K.

Introduction

The role of foreign firms in the US economy has grown rapidly over the past decade. By a variety of measures, the share of US assets, employment, and production held by US affiliates of foreign firms has increased by a factor of between two and three since 1977. This growing foreign presence has sparked a flood of popular articles and books, most of them expressing concern, and many alarm.[1] Their authors worry that foreign firms will behave differently from domestic ones in ways that reduce employment, worsen the trade deficit, or inhibit technological progress; they warn that too large a foreign presence may compromise national sovereignty or threaten national security. Relatively fewer books and articles have been devoted to a defense of foreign investment in the United States, but statements arguing generally in favor of such investment are common, usually proceeding from a general presumption in favor of free markets.[2]

Clearly, foreign direct investment (FDI) in the United States has become a major issue. Yet so far there has been a remarkable absence of serious analytical discussion of the subject. Both the critics and the defenders of FDI have relied primarily on anecdotes and *a priori* judgments rather than on systematic analysis of the data. To the extent that the debate has had a central focus at all, it has been on the assessment of employment impacts of FDI—a question that, we will argue, is misguided and sterile.

The purpose of this study is to fill this gap in the literature by presenting a more analytical discussion of the growing foreign presence in the US economy than has appeared to date. Our discussion focuses on six key questions, our answers to which are summarized here.

---

1. Recent popular treatments of the subject include Burstein (1988), Frantz and Collins (1989), Glickman and Woodward (1989), Prestowitz (1988), Rohatyn (1989), Spencer (1988), and Tolchin and Tolchin (1988).

2. See, for example, Becker (1989). More balanced discussions that are on the whole favorable to foreign direct investment are those by Morgan Guaranty (1989) and Peterson (1989).

1

- What is the extent of foreign control of US production, and how fast is it growing?

Popular treatments of FDI sometimes seem to suggest that a wholesale takeover of US assets is occurring. Since standard statistics indicate that the role of foreign firms, although growing, is still modest, the concern is either that the numbers greatly understate the actual foreign role or that the foreign presence is growing so rapidly that it will become very large in the very near future.

Chapter 1 presents and analyzes the most recent US government data on the extent and trend of inward FDI (direct investment entering the United States from abroad, as opposed to direct investment abroad by US firms, or outward FDI). By the end of 1987 foreign-owned firms, by various measures, controlled 3 to 4 percent of the US economy as a whole and 7 to 10 percent of the manufacturing sector; by 1988 foreign firms controlled 15 to 20 percent of the US banking sector. Although there are potential errors of measurement in these numbers, in both directions, such errors are unlikely to be large enough to make much difference. These numbers represent increases of about 200 percent for the US economy as a whole and about 150 percent for both the manufacturing and the banking sectors since the mid-1970s. Balance of payments statistics, however, show that the surge in FDI that began in late 1986 is continuing, so that both the overall and the manufacturing shares are presumably still rising. Thus, the foreign role in the US economy has indeed grown rapidly and is fairly substantial. However, it is still well below that in most other advanced countries.

- Why has FDI in the United States increased?

Rising concern about the role of foreign firms has coincided with the rise of foreign claims on the United States in general, associated with the unprecedented series of US current account deficits since 1981. Thus, much of the popular literature ties the growth of FDI to the US movement toward net debtor status and suggests that increasing foreign control is ultimately tied to low US savings. An alternative view is that the coincidence of current account deficits and rising concern about FDI is just that, a coincidence, and that the growing role of foreign firms in the United States has deeper roots in changes in the US role in the world economy. FDI flows in the balance of payments have increased sharply since 1986; some analysts have attributed this development to the decline in the dollar, others to changes in US corporate taxation.

Chapter 2 examines the sources of recent growth in FDI in the United States. Explanations of FDI generally fall into one of two categories: cost-of-capital explanations, which tie FDI to international capital flows generally, and industrial-organization explanations, which view FDI as dictated chiefly by corporate strategy rather than by capital movements.

The coincidence of growing inward FDI and US current account deficits since 1981 provides surface plausibility to a cost-of-capital story. However, a closer look at the facts does not support this view. US inward FDI has in fact been growing steadily since the early 1970s and grew more rapidly during the period from 1977 to 1981—before the emergence of large US current account deficits—than during the years of peak aggregate capital inflow. Also, most of the increase in foreign holdings in the United States has come from European and especially British firms, even though Great Britain has not been a large exporter of capital; Japanese FDI, although of growing importance, is still only a fraction of the story. Examination of individual industries, such as the color television and the automobile industries, confirms that when US production is undertaken by foreign firms it is typically because the foreigners have firm-specific assets that give them an advantage in management and technology, not because they have a lower cost of capital. Within the broad industrial-organization story that we believe best explains the general increase of FDI in the United States, shifts in exchange rates, taxation, and protection all probably play important roles in explaining the timing of this investment.

■ What are the economic benefits and costs of a growing foreign presence?

Much of the popular literature argues that foreign ownership will adversely affect US employment and trade or lead to a shift of good jobs and advanced technology away from the United States. Defenders of FDI suggest that it provides important gains as a result of increased global economic integration and possibly valuable external economies as well. One issue that has surfaced since the dollar began to fall in early 1985 is whether foreign firms, regardless of the long-run effect of their presence on the US economy, are being allowed to buy up US assets at bargain prices—the so-called fire sale issue. This concern was exacerbated by the October 1987 crash of the US stock market and by the continuing remarkably high level of Japanese stock prices.

The economic impact, positive and negative, of FDI is considered in Chapter 3, which argues that most concerns about harmful foreign-firm behavior are not borne out by the experience with FDI so far. US affiliates of foreign firms look quite similar to US firms in the same industries in terms of value added per worker, rates of compensation, and research and development. The main noticeable difference between foreign-owned and domestic firms is that the former do on average import substantially more of their production inputs per worker. This is particularly true of Japanese firms. The apparent higher propensity to import may in part be a statistical illusion due to misclassifications and biases in the types of activities foreign firms enter, and even on the most pessimistic assumptions, this tendency to import represents a modest cost to the

United States. Nonetheless, it may become a source of considerable tension in the future. As to the "fire sale" argument, much of this discussion is conceptually confused. To the extent that US assets are being sold at prices below their true value, the resulting loss is small even under very pessimistic assumptions.

■ What are the domestic political consequences of FDI?

Concerns have been raised that a large presence of foreign firms will distort the political process, with foreign interests carrying too much weight in domestic decisions. Defenders of FDI argue that this risk is mild and that other countries have been able to accept substantial amounts of FDI without seriously compromising their sovereignty.

Chapter 4 examines whether foreign firms exert influence on the US political process in ways that ultimately harm the interests of domestic residents. There is some valid logic behind this concern—not in that foreign firms differ qualitatively from other special interests in their behavior, but because any redistribution of income to foreign firms through the political process represents a national loss in a sense that purely internal redistribution does not. In practice, however, the costs and inefficiencies associated with even run-of-the-mill domestic special-interest politics make it difficult to get especially concerned about the additional costs arising from foreign intervention.

■ Does foreign investment threaten national security?

There is concern that the presence of foreign firms, particularly in industries that generate advanced technology, will somehow compromise US security interests; others dismiss this as a minor issue, adequately dealt with under existing rules and regulations.

We discuss the national security implications of FDI in Chapter 5. There are some serious problems to be dealt with in this area. The reason is not so much that foreign firms themselves endanger national security, but rather that existing procurement practices and regulations designed to safeguard sensitive US technologies complicate, if not preclude, contractual arrangements between the Pentagon and foreign-owned firms. As a result, there is a sense in which FDI shrinks the industrial base available for defense contracting. This is an issue that will have to be addressed as the foreign role in the US economy grows.

■ What should be done?

A variety of proposals have been offered to deal with the growth of FDI in the United States; these range from benign neglect, through proposals for stiffer reporting requirements for foreign affiliates, to demands for restrictions on foreign ownership and performance requirements for those foreign firms operating in the United States. The ultimate purpose of this study is to shed light on the merits of these proposals; in Chapter 7 we also offer a few proposals of our own.

The basic thrust of this study is that alarm about the consequences of a growing foreign presence in the US economy is not warranted. The share of the US economy controlled by foreign firms, although growing, is not exploding. The importance of foreign firms in the US economy is still considerably less than what has been more or less comfortably accepted in European countries since the early 1970s. And although foreign firms do apparently have a higher import propensity than domestic firms, the more serious charge—that foreign firms keep their high-value-added or more sophisticated activities at home—is not borne out by the evidence. Moreover, should a real threat to national security arise from the attempts of foreign firms to acquire US assets, the US government is well empowered to block such action. Indeed, ambiguities in existing law open the door to wholesale screening of foreign investment and imposition of performance requirements in a manner that would run sharply counter to the traditional US posture of neutrality toward FDI.

For these reasons, we believe that new measures that would place special burdens on foreign-owned firms that are not placed on domestic firms, including new reporting and disclosure requirements, are not appropriate. There are some difficult issues to be addressed in the defense area, but these require domestic reforms that accommodate the fact of FDI, not an effort to reverse this generally desirable trend.

Extent and Trends

Debate over foreign direct investment in the United States begins with a dispute over facts. Many critics allege that US statistics fail to measure the true extent of growing foreign ownership and control;[1] the legislative initiative most likely to be enacted in the near term, that proposed by Representative John C. Bryant (D-TX)—the so-called Bryant amendment—mandates increased reporting requirements for foreign-owned firms. Thus, we begin with a discussion of what is known about FDI and its growth in the United States.

What Is FDI?

The very definition of FDI poses serious problems. What we seek to measure is the extent to which foreign firms and individuals control US production, yet it is not easy to define precisely either the nationality of a firm or what constitutes control.

What Is the Nationality of a Firm?

Foreign direct investment is formally defined as ownership of assets by foreign residents for purposes of controlling the use of those assets. In most cases, however, the foreign "resident" is a firm—a legal but not an actual person. This raises the question of whether a firm that produces in more than one country can properly be said to have a nationality.

It is easy to come up with examples that call the whole issue of the nationality of a firm into question. In what realistic sense are Shell and British Petroleum (BP)—multinational firms with a huge stake in both the United States and Europe—more foreign than Exxon and Mobil, of which exactly the same may

---

1. Thus, Representative John D. Dingell (R-MI) asserts that "The information currently collected by the government is incomplete, inaccurate. . . . It is virtually useless to the analysis and decision making of policymakers" (foreword to Frantz and Collins 1989, ix).

be said? Admittedly, the central headquarters of Shell and BP lie in Europe, whereas those of Exxon and Mobil lie in the United States, but it is far from clear that this makes any substantial difference in the ways these firms behave. More generally, if a firm is simply conceived of as an organizational entity that sprawls across national boundaries, it does not make obvious sense to speak of the firm as a resident of any one of the countries in which any of its operations— including operation of a central headquarters—takes place.

Questioning the meaningfulness of the concept of firm nationality leads naturally to abandonment of the attempt to measure the role of foreign firms in the US economy at all. On an extreme view, we should instead simply measure the role of multinational firms, whatever their national origin. By this measure it is not at all clear that the United States is experiencing any noticeable change: if Honda comes to have a larger share of US automobile production, and General Motors a smaller share, this is simply substituting one multinational for another.

In practice we need not give up quite so easily. In our still imperfectly integrated world, firms by and large continue to have different centers of gravity that give them a more or less definable national identity. To call General Motors an American company, and Honda a Japanese one, does some violence to the fact that each is a multinational concern producing in several countries, yet Honda is clearly more Japanese, in terms of the weight of its interests and economic stake, and General Motors more American.

The nationality problem becomes most acute in defining the effective nationality of firms originating in small and medium-sized countries. Philips, SKF, and Seagram are all firms that originate in such countries (the Netherlands, Sweden, and Canada, respectively) yet do most of their production and sales elsewhere—in the case of SKF to such an extent that English rather than Swedish is the official corporate language. Since investment by Dutch and Canadian firms is a substantial part of FDI in the United States (and British firms often seem equally anational or binational), there are in fact serious definitional problems with the numbers discussed later in this chapter.

What Constitutes Control?

Direct investment is ownership that carries with it actual control over what is owned; this aspect of control distinguishes direct investment from portfolio investment, which is simply the establishment of a claim on an asset for the purpose of realizing some return. In practice, even if the intent of the investor to assert or not assert control could be objectively determined, there remains the difficulty of determining what share of ownership brings with it actual control. The US Department of Commerce defines a foreign investment as direct when a single investor has acquired a stake of 10 percent or more in a US firm. That firm is then considered a domestic affiliate of the foreign investor. The 10 percent criterion is meant to reflect the idea that a large stockholder will generally have a strong say in the operations of a company even if that stockholder does not actually have a majority stake. The requirement that the 10 percent be held by a single owner reflects the possibility that a firm may have many small foreign stockholders while remaining effectively under domestic control.

It is easy to see how this working definition could go astray in either direction, by failing to identify control exercised by foreign investors holding less than 10 percent ownership or by defining a US firm as foreign controlled when the foreign owner does not exercise real control. The question is whether these potential pitfalls are important in practice. The evidence is strong that they are not.

The potential for understating foreign control comes from the possibility that a firm with many small foreign investors may effectively act in their collective interest even though no one of them has more than a 10 percent share. Suppose, for example, that 15 Japanese residents (individuals or firms) together hold 80 percent of a US firm's shares. Even if these foreign residents do not constitute a preorganized group, management might act in a way that favors the interests of the Japanese stockholders over those of the US stockholders. This would give the foreign shareholders a measure of *de facto* control even though the US firm would not be recorded as a subsidiary of a Japanese firm.

In practice, large-scale stock ownership by foreign nationals has been less of a measurement concern than other kinds of investment, especially in real estate. Small-scale foreign investments in real estate are sometimes organized through mechanisms that effectively give control to foreign residents without the official statistics reflecting such control. In particular, limited partnerships constitute a known gap in measurement. When foreign investors buy US real estate through a limited partnership where the controlling partners are US residents, the investment is not counted as direct, because the limited partners do not have *de jure* control. In practice, however, limited partners usually do have an important say in operations. (Remarkably, foreign investments in limited partnerships do not show up as portfolio investment either; they therefore constitute a complete gap in coverage.)

Almost certainly, however, these exceptions are not of great economic importance. The potential dollar value of investments that miss being counted in this way is regarded by all of those familiar with the numbers as limited, and in any case such investments are not the ones that have caused FDI in the United States to become a major issue. What we are really interested in are the situations in which US manufacturing firms, banks, and other businesses are integrated into the control structure of foreign-based multinational firms. These cases require that a single foreign parent establish unambiguous control and are not disguisable.

What about the possibility of overstating FDI? The misclassification of some firms as foreign when they are *de facto* US–based may be a significant source of overstatement. Leaving this issue to one side, however, the main potential problem is that of large foreign investments that are not aimed at establishing operational control. Suppose that a foreign individual or firm purchases 13 percent of a US firm purely as an investment, leaving existing management in charge, the corporate headquarters in the United States, and so on. Counting this as FDI will surely overstate the extent of change in actual operational control.

There are some familiar examples of this problem. The most spectacular is that of Du Pont, 22.9 percent of which is owned by the Bronfman (Seagram) family of Canada; as a result, Du Pont is classified as a Canadian firm. Since Du Pont's operations have not been placed under control of a foreign-based chemical enterprise—and the *de facto* nationality of the owner is itself arguable, whatever the family's citizenship—this is clearly a misclassification by our standards. Indeed, the situation is even more interesting because Du Pont also qualifies as a US parent firm holding controlled affiliates abroad. We are told by the staff of the Bureau of Economic Analysis (BEA) that there are a number of other cases in which the same enterprise is classified both as foreign-owned and as a US parent. (Under confidentiality rules, the BEA cannot reveal who these firms are; we offer Du Pont as an example because it conspicuously meets BEA criteria on the basis of public information alone.)

However, in the aggregate the danger of overstatement or understatement due to these problems is small. One reason is evident from table 1.1, which shows the financial structure of US affiliates of foreign firms in 1986. As the table shows, on average the foreign parent controlled 80.2 percent of the affiliate's equity. Thus, the typical US affiliate of a foreign firm is clearly majority owned, rather than an ambiguous case in which the foreign firm holds a fractional stake. It follows that borderline cases where passive investments by foreigners are classified as FDI must be the exception rather than the rule. Preliminary calculations done by the BEA staff suggest that raising the classifying criterion to 20 percent or even 50 percent has a minor impact.

Thus, although statistical coverage of FDI is imperfect, the imperfections do not loom very large. Broadly speaking, US official data on FDI do give an accurate picture of the extent and trend of foreign investments aimed at establishing corporate control. (Appendix A further examines the nature and adequacy of the BEA data.)

The Rise of FDI: Alternative Measures

One commonly used measure of the rate at which foreign control in the US economy is increasing is the flow of FDI into the United States as measured in

Table 1.1 Financing of US affiliates of foreign firms, 1986

	Debt and current liabilities		Equity	
	Millions of dollars	Percent of total	Millions of dollars	Percent of total
Foreign parent	71,852	13.0	124,760	80.2
Other foreigners	20,882	3.7	588	0.4
US persons	459,866	83.2	30,136	19.4
Total	552,600	99.9[a]	155,485	100.0

a. Percentages do not sum to 100 because of rounding.

Source: Bureau of Economic Analysis, "Foreign Direct Investment in the United States: Operations of U.S. Affiliates of Foreign Companies" (preliminary 1986 estimates), table C-1.

the balance of payments. This inward flow measure combines purchases of equity that lead to controlling interests or expand the holdings of foreign owners who already hold a controlling interest, retained earnings of foreign-controlled firms, and net lending from parents to subsidiaries. It does not count investment by foreign-controlled firms financed by selling either debt or equity to unrelated parties, foreign or domestic, nor does it allow for increases in the value of foreign-controlled assets. Thus, the balance of payments data may understate actual increases in foreign control to a fluctuating degree. Nonetheless, the balance of payments numbers are useful because they become available more quickly than other measures. As we shall see, this is a potentially crucial point.

Figure 1.1 shows inward flows of FDI since 1973 using the balance of payments measure. These flows are expressed as a share of US GNP. There have been two major surges in this investment: the first occurred from 1978 to 1981, and the second began in late 1986.

The effect of inward flows of FDI is presumably to expand the share of the US economy that is foreign controlled. Even given an identification of some firms as foreign controlled, however, there are alternative ways of measuring the size of the foreign stake in the United States. All such measures are subject to criticism, but by looking at several alternatives we are likely to get a reasonably comprehensive view. Table 1.2 shows six measures of the role of foreign firms in the US economy based on four alternative measures: the stock of FDI as measured by cumulative investments, the assets of US affiliates of foreign firms, the employment of these affiliates, and their value added.

Figure 1.1 Foreign direct investment flows into the United States, balance of payments basis, 1973–1989

percent of GNP (four-quarter moving average)

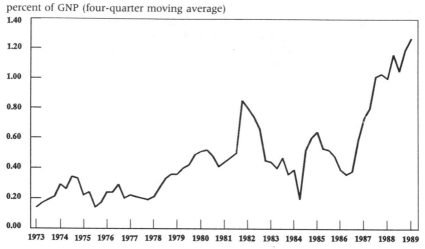

SOURCES: *Survey of Current Business,* various issues.

The Stock of FDI

The most commonly cited measure of FDI is the balance of payments–based measure of the cumulative stock of FDI in the United States. More interesting than the nominal value of this measure is a value deflated in some way that reflects inflation and economic growth, to give some idea of the extent of FDI relative to the US economy as a whole. Table 1.2 shows the FDI stock (the cumulative flow of FDI into the United States) as a percentage of the total net worth (by book value) of all nonfinancial US corporations. This FDI stock ratio more than quadrupled from 1977 to the end of 1988, when it stood at 8.9 percent.[2]

The FDI stock ratio is useful because it is easily calculated and can be brought quickly up to date, but it is not an adequate measure by itself. For one thing, because it measures book values it may understate actual market values. However, given the recency of most FDI in the United States this is a less severe problem than for US investments abroad; as Ulan and Dewald (1989) have pointed out, the market value of US direct investment abroad is probably at least twice the standard FDI stock estimate. More fundamentally, the FDI stock ratio fails to measure the extent to which foreign claims are leveraged into larger control, both through less than 100 percent ownership and through borrowing from unrelated parties. As we saw in table 1.1, the typical US affiliate of a foreign

---

2. The apparent large jump in this ratio in 1980 is due in part to a revision of the FDI data series following the 1980 benchmark survey.

Table 1.2 Role of foreign direct investment in the US economy, 1977–1988 (percentages)

Measure	1977	1978	1979	1980	1981	1982	1983	1984	1985	1986	1987	1988
FDI stock ratio[a]	2.1	2.4	2.6	3.5	4.0	3.9	4.2	4.8	5.3	6.3	7.6	8.9
Foreign share of US mfg.[b]	5.2	5.7	6.6	7.2	9.6	9.8	10.1	10.2	10.8	11.4	12.2	n.a.
Foreign share of US employment[c]	1.7	1.9	2.2	2.6	3.0	3.1	3.2	3.3	3.3	3.4	3.5	n.a.
Foreign share of mfg employment[d]	3.5	3.9	4.8	5.5	6.5	6.6	7.2	7.1	7.6	7.3	7.9	n.a.
Foreign share of GNP[e]	1.7	1.9	2.2	2.6	3.3	3.3	3.3	3.5	3.5	3.4	n.a.	n.a.
Foreign share of mfg. value added[f]	3.7	4.1	4.8	5.5	7.6	7.8	8.1	8.4	8.3	8.3	n.a.	n.a.

mfg. = manufacturing; n.a. = base data not available.

a. FDI stock ratio equals FDI stock as percentage of total net worth of nonfinancial corporations. *Sources:* FDI stock—"Foreign Direct Investment in the United States: Detail for Position and Balance of Payments Flows, 1987," *Survey of Current Business* 68 (August 1988), 69; net worth of nonfinancial corporations—Federal Reserve Board, "Balance Sheets for the U.S. Economy 1949–88," April 1989. The figure for 1988 is based on preliminary data.

b. Assets of foreign mfg. affiliates as percentage of assets of US mfg. corporations (excluding petroleum refining). *Sources:* assets of foreign mfg. affiliates—Bureau of Economic Analysis, "Foreign Direct Investment in the United States: Operations of U.S. Affiliates of Foreign Companies" (FDIUS:OUSAFC), various issues, table B-1; assets of US mfg. corporations—Bureau of the Census and Federal Trade Commission, "Quarterly Financial Report for Manufacturing, Mining, and Trade Corporations," various issues and tables.

c. Employment of foreign affiliates as percentage of total US employment. *Sources:* employment of foreign affiliates—FDIUS:OUSAFC, various issues, table F-1; US employment: "National Income and Product Accounts," *Survey of Current Business,* various issues and supplementary volume.

d. Employment of foreign mfg. affiliates as percentage of total US employment. *Sources:* employment of foreign affiliates—FDIUS:OUSAFC, various issues, table F-1; US manufacturing employment: "National Income and Product Accounts," *Survey of Current Business,* various issues and supplementary volume.

e. Output of foreign affiliates as percentage of total US GNP. *Sources:* output of foreign affiliates—Bureau of Economic Analysis, "Foreign Direct Investment in the United States: Gross Product of Nonbank U.S. Affiliates of Foreign Companies, 1977–1986" (FDIUS: GPN), 23, table 1; US GNP—"National Income and Product Accounts," *Survey of Current Business,* various issues and supplementary volume.

f. Mfg. value added of foreign affiliates as percentage of total US mfg. value added. *Sources:* mfg. value added of foreign affiliates—FDIUS:GPN, 23, table 1; US mfg. value added—"National Income and Product Accounts," *Survey of Current Business,* various issues and supplementary volume.

firm is in fact largely financed with credit from US residents, so that the FDI stock ratio could represent a serious understatement of foreign control.

Assets of Foreign Affiliates

A natural alternative to using the stock of foreign equity as a measure of FDI is to compare the assets of foreign-controlled firms with the assets of the US business sector generally. Unfortunately, total assets are dominated by those of financial firms, which do not carry with them comparable value added or employment and thus can give a misleading picture of the extent of foreign control. A reasonably valid approach, however, is to look at the assets of foreign-controlled manufacturing firms alone relative to those of all US manufacturers. (Petroleum refining, which is highly capital-intensive and has a disproportionate foreign presence, is excluded from these series.) The ratios thus calculated are each year substantially above the FDI stock ratio; as we will see shortly, however, this primarily reflects the fact that foreign firms have a larger role in the US manufacturing sector than in the rest of the economy. The other notable difference is that the asset ratio has grown more slowly than the FDI stock ratio, especially since 1981. At the end of 1987, assets of US affiliates of foreign-controlled firms in the manufacturing sector amounted to 12.2 percent of total US manufacturing assets.

Employment by Foreign Affiliates

An arguably better measure of actual foreign control is the share of the US work force employed by foreign-controlled firms. Table 1.2 shows employment in US affiliates of foreign firms as a share of total US employment, part time and full time, for the economy as a whole and for manufacturing alone (less petroleum refining), respectively. The aggregate number is roughly equal to the FDI stock ratio by the end of the series, but it starts a little higher and therefore grows more slowly. The manufacturing employment ratio is consistently somewhat smaller than the manufacturing asset share but grows at about the same rate. One should note that the growth of the manufacturing share results both from increases in the number of employees of US affiliates engaged in manufacturing and from a decline in the total US manufacturing work force.

These series highlight the substantially larger role of foreign firms in manufacturing than in the economy generally. They also reveal that the time pattern of growth in the foreign presence is not a simple trend; instead there was a surge in the late 1970s and early 1980s followed by a deceleration of growth from 1982 to 1986. Growth resumed in 1987, corresponding to the renewed surge in investment flows that we saw in figure 1.1.

Value Added by Foreign Affiliates

An alternative measure of the foreign role in the US economy is the value added by US affiliates of foreign firms as a share of value added for the US economy as a whole. Table 1.2 presents data on the share of foreign-controlled firms in value added (GNP) for the overall US economy and in the manufacturing sector alone (again excluding petroleum refining). These ratios look similar to the corresponding employment data ratios: in 1986 foreign-controlled firms were estimated to account for 3.4 percent of both US GNP and US total employment, with substantially higher levels, 8.3 and 7.3 percent, respectively, in manufacturing. However, the deceleration of growth that we observed in the employment data is even more marked in these value-added numbers; in the aggregate, growth in the foreign share virtually stops after 1981. There may well have been a resumption of growth more recently; unfortunately, however, these data are available only through 1986.

The major surprise in these data is that, by all the measures, the rate of increase in FDI in the United States was substantially more rapid before 1981–82 than from 1982 to late 1986; in particular, measures based directly on the activities of foreign firms rather than on financial measures show a distinct flattening of the trend after 1981. This striking fact is very apparent in figures 1.2 and 1.3, which present the same series graphically, in the aggregate and for the manufacturing sector, respectively.

Part of the discrepancy between the non–balance of payments measures and the FDI stock ratio can be explained by the fact that certain foreign firms have been increasing their stake in their own subsidiaries; this shows up in the data as an FDI flow but does not increase the share of foreign firms in the US economy. For example, in 1985 Shell acquired the remaining 30.5 percent of its US affiliate, converting it to a wholly owned subsidiary. Similarly, in 1987 BP acquired the remaining 45 percent of its US affiliate. In each case the extent of control by foreign firms, as measured by share of employment or value added, did not change, but the outlay of funds was presumably reported as an FDI flow.

Another factor explaining this discrepancy is found in the pattern of recent FDI, which has been biased toward highly capital-intensive activities like banking and finance, in which employment and value added per unit of capital are low. Banking in particular constitutes an important special case and is treated separately later in this chapter.

One basic message of the data, in any case, seems to be that although there has been a major increase in the role of foreign firms in the US economy, the growth of this role actually slowed sharply as the United States plunged into massive current account deficit. This seemingly paradoxical observation will play a key role in our interpretation of the causes of FDI.

Figure 1.2   Measures of the share of foreign affiliates in the overall US economy, 1977–1988

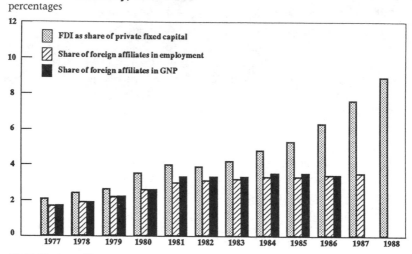

SOURCE: See table 1.2.

The major problem with these data is that they do not come fully up to the present; thus, they fail to provide as much information as we would like on the consequences of the surge in some measures of inward FDI on the extent of foreign control in the US economy. The flow of inward FDI as measured by the balance of payments accounts, shown in figure 1.1, surged sharply from the fourth quarter of 1986. Also, as table 1.3 shows, there was a surge in foreign acquisitions and establishments in 1987 and 1988, arising primarily from the activities of Japanese firms. The increase was largely in finance and banking, however, where assets are very large relative to capital and even larger relative to employment and value added. Thus, it is not clear how much of a surge there has been in foreign control of the US economy generally. The foreign presence is substantial, especially in manufacturing, and it is growing, but the extent and rate of growth should not be exaggerated.

The Mechanics of FDI

In principle, growth of the foreign presence in the US economy could take place in either of two ways. Foreign firms could grow primarily through the construction of new, "greenfield" production facilities in the United States, financed either through establishment of new subsidiaries or through invest-

Figure 1.3   Measures of the share of foreign affiliates in US manufacturing, 1977–1987

percentages

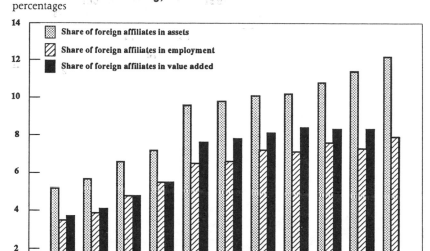

- ▒ Share of foreign affiliates in assets
- ▨ Share of foreign affiliates in employment
- ■ Share of foreign affiliates in value added

SOURCE: See table 1.2.

ment by existing US affiliates of foreign firms. Alternatively, foreign control could grow through acquisition of existing US firms.

Obviously both kinds of growth are taking place: such ventures as the opening of new Japanese automobile plants in the United States are occurring simultaneously with such events as Seagram's acquisition of Tropicana. In quantitative terms, however, acquisitions are clearly the larger source of growth in foreign control. Table 1.4 shows some indicative numbers. The table first compares the actual investment outlays by foreign firms either to acquire or to establish subsidiaries in the United States. In most years the value of acquisitions has been several times that of new establishments. Next the table shows the value of all US enterprises acquired or established by foreign firms; this is a much larger number because it includes noncontrolling claims such as minority shareholdings and debt that is not owed to the parent. This number is considerably larger than total expenditure on new plant and equipment by US affiliates of foreign firms (next item in table 1.4). If one bears in mind that this is gross rather than net investment, it becomes clear that acquisitions have been the dominant source of growth. One should think of Campeau's purchase of Federated Department Stores, not Honda's opening of its Marysville, Ohio, plant, as the characteristic way in which FDI has grown.

Table 1.3 Asset value of US business enterprises acquired or established by foreign firms, 1980–1988 (billions of dollars)

Year	All industries	Banking and finance	Japan
1980	49.7	29.0	n.a.
1981	87.7	39.3	n.a.
1982	31.9	11.8	1.1
1983	22.3	11.3	0.8
1984	40.5	17.3	7.4
1985	36.1	7.4	2.0
1986	71.8	18.1	11.2
1987	131.1	83.4	75.3
1988[a]	126.8	23.2	25.9

n.a. = not available.

a. Data for 1988 are preliminary.

Sources: For 1987 and 1988, "U.S. Businesses Acquired or Established by Foreign Direct Investors in 1988," *Survey of Current Business* 69 (May 1989), tables 6A, 6B, and supplementary table 17; data for 1980–86 from similar articles in *Survey of Current Business* (May, various years).

The Role of Japan

For a number of reasons, Japanese direct investment in the United States has attracted special attention. Japanese firms have been the most spectacular competitors to US–based corporations, and there is naturally curiosity and concern about whether they can repeat their successes in the United States. Japan has also been the principal exporter of portfolio capital in the 1980s—in effect the principal source of financing for the US current account deficit—and some have asked whether Japanese investors will continue to accept a passive role. Finally, there is a general sense that Japanese firms may behave differently from other foreign firms, either because of their protected domestic base or because they have a different culture and institutional structure.

We address the question of differences in behavior in later chapters. For now, the major point is the relatively small but rapidly increasing role of Japanese firms in many measures of US inward FDI. Table 1.5 shows seven measures of the share of Japanese firms in the overall foreign presence in the United States: their share of the FDI stock, their shares of foreign-held assets in the aggregate and in manufacturing (excluding petroleum refining), their shares of employment by foreign firms in the aggregate and in manufacturing, and their shares of value added by foreign firms in the aggregate and in manufacturing. Despite the marked upward trend, Japan remains a relatively minor player in the total FDI

Table 1.4 Sources of growth in foreign control of US firms, 1981–1988
(billions of dollars)

	1980	1981	1982	1983	1984	1985	1986	1987	1988
Investment in									
Acquisitions	18.2	6.6	4.8	11.8	20.1	31.5	25.6	33.9	60.0
Establishments	5.1	4.3	3.2	3.4	3.0	7.7	4.9	6.4	5.0
Assets of firms established or acquired	87.7	31.9	22.3	40.5	36.1	71.8	111.2	131.1	126.8
Investment in new plant and equipment	26.7	28.1	23.2	25.2	28.9	28.3	n.a.	n.a.	n.a.

n.a. = not available.

Source: "U.S. Business Enterprises Acquired or Established by Foreign Direct Investors in 1988," *Survey of Current Business* 68 (May 1988), tables 3, 6A, and 6B (and equivalent articles in previous May issues).

picture, as measured by its share of employment and value added, and is especially underrepresented in manufacturing. The large Japanese acquisitions and establishments in 1987 and 1988, shown in table 1.3, have increased the Japanese asset share in recent data; indeed, assets of firms classified as Japanese-controlled doubled in 1987. As we have noted, however, these increases took place primarily in financial firms, where large assets carry with them control over only small value added and employment.

The key point is that the rise in FDI in the United States is not an essentially Japanese phenomenon. One way to make the point is to look at the raw employment numbers. From 1977 to 1987, the number of workers employed by US affiliates of foreign firms increased by 1.6 million, but only 200,000 of these employees were in Japanese-controlled firms.

Banking

The banking sector constitutes a special case, in which the numbers look quite different from those for other forms of FDI. The leveling off of the foreign role after the early 1980s that is apparent in the aggregate data did not happen in banking, where the share of foreign ownership in total assets (but not in loans or deposits) continued to rise rapidly. Also, Japanese firms dominate FDI in banking, in contrast to manufacturing and other sectors.

Foreign banks can operate in the United States in three forms: branches, agencies, and subsidiaries. (In New York State there is a fourth form, investment

Table 1.5 Japanese share of foreign direct investment in the United States, 1977–1988 (percentages)

Share of:	1977	1978	1979	1980	1981	1982	1983	1984	1985	1986	1987	1988
Total FDI stock[a]	5.0	6.5	6.4	5.1	6.4	7.8	8.3	9.0	10.5	12.2	12.9	16.2
Total assets[b]	11.8	12.2	10.6	9.5	8.0	7.5	7.3	8.6	8.7	11.7	21.1	n.a.
Mfg. assets[b]	4.8	4.8	5.0	4.7	4.0	4.2	4.5	5.8	6.1	5.8	n.a.	n.a.
Total employ-ment[c]	6.3	6.3	6.0	5.7	5.7	5.7	6.4	7.0	7.4	7.5	9.0	n.a.
Mfg. employ-ment[c]	3.1	3.4	3.6	3.3	3.7	3.6	4.0	4.7	5.1	5.0	5.4	n.a.
Total value added[d]	7.1	6.7	6.9	7.0	6.6	7.0	7.4	9.1	10.1	9.7	n.a.	n.a.
Mfg. value added[d]	3.4	3.7	3.7	3.4	3.5	3.0	3.7	4.6	5.0	4.9	n.a.	n.a.

mfg. = manufacturing; n.a. = base data not available.

Sources:

a. For 1977–87: "Foreign Direct Investment in the United States: Detail of Position and Balance of Payments Flows," *Survey of Current Business* (August, various years); for 1988 (preliminary): Bureau of Economic Analysis, "Growth in Foreign Direct Investment in the United States Outpaced That of U.S. Direct Investment Abroad in 1988," US Department of Commerce news release (BEA 89–31), 29 June 1989.

b. Bureau of Economic Analysis, "Foreign Direct Investment in the United States: Operations of U.S. Affiliates of Foreign Companies" (FDIUS:OUSAFC), various issues, table B-7.

c. FDIUS:OUSAFC, various issues, table F-4.

d. Bureau of Economic Analysis, "Foreign Direct Investment in the United States: Gross Product of Nonbank U.S. Affiliates of Foreign Companies, 1977–86," table 3.

Table 1.6 Assets, loans, and deposits of US financial affiliates of foreign banks and bank holding companies, 1973–1988[a]

Year	Billions of dollars			Percentage of total for all US banks		
	Assets	Loans	Deposits	Assets	Loans	Deposits
1973	32.3	17.6	11.4	3.8	3.7	1.7
1974	46.1	27.0	17.0	4.9	5.1	2.3
1975	52.4	29.9	22.6	5.3	5.7	2.9
1976	61.3	35.4	26.1	5.8	6.4	3.1
1977	76.8	41.5	22.8	6.4	6.6	2.4
1978	109.1	65.3	46.3	8.0	8.8	4.4
1979	149.6	91.9	62.8	9.9	10.9	5.6
1980	200.6	121.4	80.4	11.9	13.4	6.6
1981	250.6	157.7	101.8	13.5	15.4	7.7
1982	299.8	185.2	154.3	14.4	16.3	10.4
1983	328.8	192.4	181.3	14.6	15.6	11.1
1984	394.4	220.1	233.7	15.9	15.1	12.9
1985	440.8	247.4	236.7	16.1	15.4	12.1
1986	524.3	276.9	278.2	17.3	15.6	12.8
1987	592.6	310.9	316.1	19.0	16.6	14.1
1988	615.4	320.6	303.5	19.2	16.6	13.4

a. Data for 1973–87 are as of the last Wednesday of the year; those for 1988 as of the last Wednesday of June. Affiliates include branches, agencies, and banking subsidiaries.

Source: Federal Reserve Board data base.

companies, but these appear to be a minor factor.) The distinctions among these forms of ownership need not concern us here. Table 1.6 shows several measures of the role of foreign banks' branches, agencies, and subsidiaries in the US banking sector. Overall, the foreign role in this sector has grown at about the same rate as in the economy as a whole, but the foreign presence has consistently been much larger than in other sectors. Another special feature of the banking sector is the importance of Japan; whereas in other sectors Japan is generally a minority presence, table 1.7 shows that Japanese banks account for more than half the assets of foreign banks in the United States.

Clearly the banking sector is an exception to several of our generalizations about FDI in the United States. We discuss some of the reasons for this different behavior in Chapter 2.

Real Estate

Of all aspects of FDI in the United States, the ownership of US real estate by foreigners has emerged as one of the most sensitive. Some of this sensitivity has

Table 1.7 Assets of US affiliates of foreign banks and bank holding companies, by country, 1988[a]

| Country | US banking assets of foreign affiliates | | |
	Billions of dollars	As percentage of US banking assets held by foreign banks	As percentage of total US banking assets
Japan	321.5	52.2	10.1
Canada	44.0	7.1	1.4
United Kingdom	41.4	6.7	1.3
Italy	37.8	6.1	1.2
France	26.9	4.4	0.8
Hong Kong	26.6	4.3	0.8
Switzerland	22.6	3.7	0.7
Germany	13.5	2.2	0.4
Netherlands	10.2	1.7	0.3
Israel	8.5	1.4	0.3
Ireland	6.2	1.0	0.2
Spain	5.9	1.0	0.2
Mexico	4.2	0.7	0.1
Brazil	4.1	0.7	0.1
Korea	4.1	0.7	0.1
Australia	3.5	0.6	0.1
Belgium	2.7	0.4	0.1
Taiwan	2.7	0.4	0.1
Venezuela	2.3	0.4	0.1
Denmark	1.9	0.3	0.1
Indonesia	1.9	0.3	0.1
Austria	1.3	0.2	0.0
Greece	1.2	0.2	0.0
Norway	1.2	0.2	0.0
Luxembourg	1.1	0.2	0.0
All others	18.1	2.9	0.6
Total	615.4	100.0	19.2

a. Data are as of the last day of June 1988. Affiliates include branches, agencies, and banking subsidiaries.

Source: Federal Reserve Board data base.

to do with the fact that foreign ownership of US real estate seems to be heavily concentrated in a relatively small number of locations: Hawaii, downtown Los Angeles and Houston, and some other major urban areas. However, emotional articles regarding foreign ownership of urban real estate have appeared in the popular press even in areas where this ownership does not seem to represent a particularly large percentage of the total; see, for example, a recent article in *Boston* magazine (Jahnke 1989).

Also contributing to this increased sensitivity is the widespread belief that there is a great deal of unreported foreign ownership of US real estate. This is a difficult question to deal with, for three reasons. First, the BEA readily admits that there may be some underreporting of small holdings of US real estate by nonresident foreigners. If so, it is largely a matter of ignorance on the part of the investors themselves. For example, a private Japanese citizen who buys a residential property in a major US city to hold as a personal investment may not know that he or she is legally obligated to report the holding to the BEA; indeed, the real estate agent who arranges the purchase may be just as ignorant of this requirement as the client. However, analysts we have interviewed doubt that the aggregate value of real estate held by foreigners that is unreported for this reason amounts to more than 1 to 2 percent of total reported foreign real estate holdings. A second factor that complicates measurement in this area is a loophole in US reporting requirements that allows certain limited partnerships created to hold real estate to escape reporting altogether. US officials are investigating this loophole, and the total number of cases involved is estimated to be quite small. A third problem is deliberate evasion of reporting requirements; the best-known cases are those of the family of Ferdinand Marcos and of members of the Medellín (Colombia) cocaine cartel. Again, although the stories are real, their aggregate significance is doubtful.

What is known about foreign real estate holdings in the United States? First, like all other categories of inward FDI, they have grown quite rapidly in recent years. The National Association of Realtors estimates that these holdings more than doubled in value, from $11.4 billion to $24.5 billion, from 1982 to 1987. The BEA reports that total assets held by US affiliates of foreigners classified as being in the real estate industry totaled $67.8 billion at the end of 1986, which is considerably higher than the National Association of Realtors figure. BEA data also indicate that foreign investors owned almost 15 million acres of US land at the end of 1986. As always, the BEA asset figures are stated at book value, and hence it is not quite correct to compare them with the market value of all US real estate at the end of 1986. At any rate the BEA asset figures do not include the value of real estate held by US affiliates not classified as in the real estate industry; these affiliates accounted for over 85 percent of the total foreign ownership of US acreage at the end of 1986.

The 15 million acres owned by foreigners represent less than two-thirds of 1 percent of all the land in the United States, although it is almost surely true that the percentage share of foreign-owned land among high-valued properties (such as urban real estate or high-grade farmland) in the United States is greater. Indeed, given the concentration of foreign holdings in urban land areas, one might suppose that the foreign share of US real estate by value is much higher than the share of acreage. However, the figures that we have been able to obtain do not show this. The Federal Reserve Board estimates that the total value of real estate in the United States at the end of 1987 was $9,489 billion. The National Association of Realtors figure divided by the Federal Reserve Board figure suggests that, by value, foreigners held only 0.25 percent of US real estate in 1987. When the BEA number is used as the numerator, this ratio rises to 0.7 percent. These percentages clearly are not precise: the National Association of Realtors figure for market value is surely too low, and the BEA number is misleading for the reasons noted. Nonetheless, even if these numbers are off by as much as a factor of ten, it would appear that foreign holdings of US real estate as a percentage of the total are less than the foreign presence in the economy as a whole. Indeed, the data all suggest that the foreign presence in US real estate is very small.

The MIT Center for Real Estate Development has performed detailed studies of foreign investment in US real estate in six major cities: Los Angeles, Honolulu, Chicago, Phoenix, Atlanta, and Washington (Bacow 1987, 1988). Two points in particular seem worth noting. First, the bulk of foreign acquisitions of real estate in these cities has been by passive investors who hold the assets as portfolio investments for income and capital appreciation rather than as direct investments. Second, the preference of foreign investors for "show-case" investments tends to give these investments greater visibility than their overall importance warrants. To take the most extreme example, more than two-thirds of the office space in downtown Los Angeles is owned by foreigners, yet the percentage of foreign-owned office space in the whole of the Los Angeles metropolitan area is quite small (although it is growing as predominantly Japanese investors gain more experience in the overall Los Angeles market).

FDI in Other Countries

A useful way to assess the growing role of foreign-controlled firms in the US economy is to compare the US experience with FDI with that of other countries. As we noted at the beginning, concerns about FDI are new only in the United States. Other countries, including other advanced countries, have long had a substantial foreign presence. It is arguable that the United States is simply becoming more normal—that it is becoming, like other nations, a host as well as a home for multinational firms.

International comparisons of FDI are difficult because the data are scarce and often noncomparable. Table 1.8 presents some estimates, prepared by Julius and Thomsen (1988), showing shares of foreign-owned firms in sales, manufacturing employment, and assets in the Group of Five countries for 1977 and

Table 1.8 Measures of the role of foreign direct investment in the economies of the Group of Five countries, 1977 and 1986
(percentages)

Share of foreign-owned firms	1977	1986
United States		
Sales	5	10
Mfg. employment	3	7
Assets	5	9
Japan		
Sales	2	1
Mfg. employment	2	1
Assets	2	1
France		
Sales	24	27
Mfg. employment	18	21
Assets	n.a.	n.a.
Germany		
Sales	17	18
Mfg. employment	14	13
Assets	17	17
United Kingdom		
Sales	22	20
Mfg. employment	15	14
Assets	n.a.	14

n.a. = not available.

Source: D. Julius and S. Thomsen, "Foreign-owned Firms, Trade, and Economic Integration," *Tokyo Club Papers* 2. London: Royal Institute of International Affairs, 1988.

1986. Their estimates for the United States differ slightly from our own and are not perfectly comparable across countries, but they are useful as indicators and tell a suggestive and credible story.

That story is essentially one of convergence. In 1977, the United States had an exceptionally small amount of inward FDI; much of the rise between then and now can be viewed as a shift to a more typical position. This was a specifically US phenomenon, not part of a global trend toward increased internationalization of business; indeed, there was essentially no trend in the relative importance of foreign firms in the other major countries.

Despite the rapid growth in the role of foreign firms in the United States, in 1986 such firms were still only about half as important as in the typical large European country. The United States is, however, much larger than any of the

European countries, and one would expect a somewhat smaller foreign role as a result. To put it another way, interregional investment that appears as domestic in the United States is recorded as international in Europe. In France about half of the foreign share in sales, employment, and assets consists of firms from other European nations (although France is exceptional in this regard). Thus, the role of foreign firms in the United States, while still less than that in Europe, has converged to a considerable degree with the European situation.

If the United States is in the process of becoming more or less ordinary with regard to foreign penetration, Japan remains a marked outlier, with very little foreign role in the economy as compared with other industrial countries. This presumably reflects a long history of controls over FDI, which have only recently been relaxed, together with the familiar yet elusive cultural and institutional barriers that make access to the Japanese market difficult for exporters and investors alike.

Conclusions

Since the mid-1970s, there has been a major qualitative change in the role of the United States with respect to multinational enterprise. Instead of being primarily a home country with little domestic production by foreign firms, the United States is now, like most other advanced countries, both a home and a host to multinationals on a significant scale. The foreign presence still represents a small fraction of overall US output and employment, but it is more prominent in the manufacturing sector and quite considerable in the banking sector.

Three common perceptions about FDI in the United States are not borne out by the data. First, the growing foreign role is not primarily a US–Japan issue. Except in banking, Japanese firms account for only a small fraction of both the level of foreign presence and its growth, although they have increased considerably in relative importance.

Second, the data do not suggest that the rate of growth of foreign firms in the US economy accelerated in tandem with the emergence of large US current account deficits after 1981. If anything, most measures suggest a leveling off of FDI after 1981 or 1982, following a surge in the 1977–81 period. There has been a renewed surge in FDI since 1986, but the extent to which foreign control has actually been extended is still unclear.

Third, foreign investors do not own a large fraction of US real estate. By several measures, the foreign presence in this sector seems to be significantly lower than in the economy as a whole. This statement remains true even under the assumption that the reported aggregate figures for foreign ownership of US real estate significantly understate the true amount of this ownership.

2

Sources of Growth

The Theory of FDI

As a starting point for any understanding of the rising role of foreign-controlled firms in the US economy, at least a rough theoretical framework is necessary. Although there is a very large literature on the causes of foreign direct investment, for the purposes of this study many of the issues raised there may be neglected. Instead we focus on a few key points, and in particular on a distinction between two competing classes of explanations.

This distinction may be made with a simplified example. Imagine that an existing US factory could be acquired by either a US–based or a foreign-based firm and that this factory is expected to yield a constant annual cash flow in perpetuity. Why might the foreign firm be willing to pay more for the factory than the domestic firm? There are two possible reasons: either the foreign firm might expect to achieve a larger annual cash flow—that is, the factory might be more profitable in foreign hands—or it might value any given cash flow more highly because it has a lower cost of capital.

The same logic obviously applies when considering who will build a new factory or expand existing facilities. When foreign rather than domestic firms do so it is either because they expect higher returns or because they require lower returns.

Let us first ask why the factory might be more profitable—earn higher returns—in foreign hands. The bulk of the FDI literature is concerned with this question. There is a presumption that, other things being equal, domestic firms should have an advantage in producing on their own home ground. There are then a wide variety of explanations for how this presumed domestic advantage may be offset. The foreign firm may have some firm-specific knowledge or assets that enable it simply to do a better job of managing. The apparently superior production-management skills of Japanese automobile manufacturers are an example. Alternatively, the US factory may be of greater value to the foreign firm because it has a potential role in that firm's global strategy that it does not have for the US firm. For example, if there are strong advantages to vertical integration, foreign suppliers of upstream inputs may value downstream plants in the United States more than their domestic rivals do. Or firms may need to produce in the United States in order to appropriate the gains from their activities elsewhere—in research and development, for example. In general, we may characterize all the reasons why a factory in the United States might be worth more to a foreign-based firm than to a domestic firm as "industrial-organization" explanations of FDI.

On the other hand, foreign firms might be no better than US firms at producing and might receive no other special payoff from controlling US production, yet be willing to pay more for US factories simply because they have a lower discount rate. This may be referred to as the "cost-of-capital" explanation of FDI. To the extent that the cost-of-capital explanation is correct, the motivation for FDI is similar to that for foreign investment in general: it is simply a matter of resources in search of the highest return.

The consensus in the academic literature on FDI since the seminal early work of Hymer (1959) has been that industrial-organization considerations rather than costs of capital explain most FDI. (A brief survey of this literature is given in Appendix B.) FDI is essentially a means to extend control for reasons of corporate strategy, rather than a channel for shifting resources from one country to another. In other words, the "investment" component of FDI is actually the least important part of the story.

Several arguments are typically offered in support of this view. First, investors simply seeking a higher return can achieve that aim through portfolio investments in securities rather than by the more cumbersome route of corporate direct investment, so that the cost-of-capital view fails to explain why the direct rather than the portfolio route should be chosen. Second, firms engaging in FDI often finance an important share of the investment locally; it is hard to understand why they would do this if a low cost of capital at home were the motivation for investing in the first place. Third, FDI among advanced countries proceeds in both directions, sometimes in the same industry. This is difficult to account for if differences in the cost of capital are the reason for FDI.

These arguments have led the majority of economists studying FDI to dismiss cost-of-capital explanations and focus on industrial-organization motivations for the formation of multinational enterprises. However, the recent experience of the United States has given new life to the cost-of-capital approach, at least in popular discussion. The growing concern about foreign firms in the United States has coincided with the plunge of the United States into net debtor status, and since 1980 the rates of growth of the stock of FDI and of total foreign claims on the United States have been similar. Thus, it is natural to suspect that the growth of FDI in the United States is tied to the same factors that have led to a growth in US indebtedness generally. Furthermore, anecdotes about foreign (especially Japanese) investors stress the high prices of foreign stocks and the high values of foreign currencies relative to those in the United States, which make US assets seem cheap by foreign standards. This is, in effect, a cost-of-capital argument.

It is possible to offer a sophisticated cost-of-capital argument for FDI, based on imperfections in capital markets and in corporate organization. Suppose that the following assumptions are true: debt is cheaper than equity; firms are constrained in their debt-equity ratios; and management regards internally generated funds as cheaper than new equity. Then at least some firms will borrow as much as they can and invest all their internal cash flow, but will neither issue new equity nor pay more dividends than necessary to pacify stockholders. Since they are constrained in their borrowing, such firms will have individual costs of capital that vary with their internal supplies of funds and their firm-specific investment opportunities. That is, the discount rate used in valuing investments becomes a firm-specific rather than an economy-wide value.

This approach can help explain some of the seeming paradoxes with the cost-of-capital view. First, firms will prefer to undertake their own foreign investment rather than pay large dividends and allow their stockholders to invest in foreign firms; thus, the choice of direct instead of portfolio investment is explained. Second, the firms may well want to borrow, and if the costs of debt are similar they may borrow in the host country, especially if this is viewed as a way to reduce exchange risk. Third, differences across industries together with limits to diversification can explain two-way FDI. In one industry, firms in Europe may have plenty of cash flow but few local investment opportunities, and therefore invest in the United States; in another industry the reverse may be true. The firms could instead try to invest across industries in their home countries, but management often seems to believe that it is easier to invest in a familiar industry abroad than to get into a new one at home.

Intraindustry two-way investment still cannot be explained by this view, but a sophisticated cost-of-capital explanation is at least a contender for explaining a significant fraction of FDI. The important point for the US experience is that the cost-of-capital view offers a possible link between the United States' shift to debtor status and the rise of FDI. If a decline in US savings and a perceived rise in investment opportunities in the United States led to a rise in the cost of capital generally relative to that abroad, the same divergence would presumably occur in the firm-specific costs of capital to US and foreign firms. Thus, foreign firms would be willing to bid more for US assets, and the rise in foreign participation would be linked to the US current account deficit.

Does the distinction between industrial-organization and cost-of-capital stories have any importance for policy? If FDI in the United States is primarily motivated by industrial-organization considerations, its link with growing foreign debt is largely a coincidence; it might well continue to increase sharply even if the United States were to balance its national accounts. On the other

Figure 2.1 Ratio of foreign direct investment stock in the United States to US GNP, 1972–1988

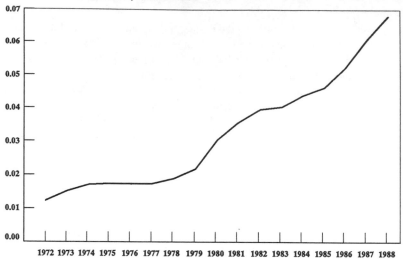

SOURCES: *Survey of Current Business,* various issues.

hand, if FDI is linked to capital flows, future FDI flows may depend crucially on the prospects for the US current account.

The next step must be to look at some evidence on the behavior of FDI in the United States. We will argue that the evidence, when looked at carefully, suggests that the industrial-organization motivation dominates the cost-of-capital motive. This implies that the apparent coincidence of rising FDI and growing debt in the 1980s is indeed simply a coincidence, and that the future growth of FDI may have little to do with the US balance of payments.

Evidence on FDI in the United States

The basic question in assessing the rise of FDI in the United States is whether this rise is a side effect of the general shift of the United States into net debtor status or whether it represents a longer-term trend driven by other factors. The widespread assumption that the debtor role and growing foreign control are linked comes from the brute fact that since 1980 large increases in FDI and US debt in general have gone together, and from the fact that Japan has simultaneously moved into a position as a large creditor and become a large direct investor in the United States. However, three less obvious facts, in our view, call

Figure 2.2 Ratio of US direct investment stock abroad to foreign direct investment stock in the United States, 1972–1988

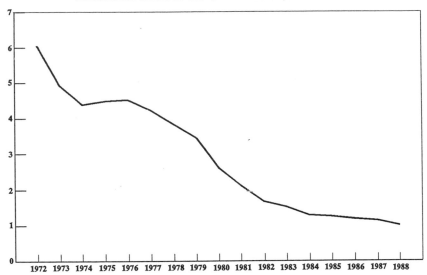

SOURCES: *Survey of Current Business,* various issues; *US Department of Commerce News,* 29 June 1989.

into question the linkage between capital flows and FDI. First, FDI in the United States has been rising rapidly for an extended period, beginning well before the emergence of US current account deficits. Second, for much of that period the driving force behind growing FDI was not the growth of foreign assets in the United States generally as much as a shift in composition of foreign claims away from portfolio investments toward FDI. Third, the national composition of FDI in the United States has consistently been one that makes no sense if FDI is viewed chiefly as a particular way of transferring capital between countries.

Figure 2.1 shows the long-term trend of the FDI stock in the United States, measured as a share of GNP.

This share has been rising steadily since the early 1970s. A simple trend fits the data quite well, and there is no evident acceleration in the rate of growth in the 1980s. Of course, since the base has grown over time, the absolute increases in the foreign presence have been larger in recent years. What is clear, however, is that unlike the net debtor status of the United States, the growth in FDI represents a long-term trend, not a development that appeared after 1981.

The change in the United States' net FDI position is also part of a long-term trend. Figure 2.2 shows one simple measure of this net position, namely, the ratio of the stock of US direct investment abroad to FDI stock in the United States. In 1970, of course, the United States was overwhelmingly a home

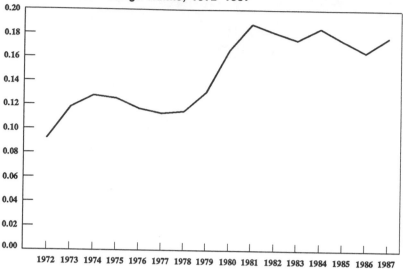

Figure 2.3 Ratio of foreign direct investment stock in the United States to total foreign claims, 1972–1987[a]

a. Data for 1987 are preliminary.

SOURCES: *Survey of Current Business*, various issues; *US Department of Commerce News*, 29 June 1989.

country rather than a host country for multinational enterprises, with an FDI stock abroad five times as large as the foreign stock in the United States. The transformation of this position, with the United States converging toward a more typical advanced-country situation as both home and host, was proceeding steadily even during the 1970s, when the United States on average was running slight surpluses on current account.

The increasing role of the United States as a host country did not for the most part have as its counterpart a general increase in foreign ownership of US assets. Instead, until the surge in foreign portfolio investment after 1981, the chief mechanism of FDI growth was a shift in the composition of foreign claims away from portfolio toward direct investment. Figure 2.3, a graph of the ratio of FDI to total foreign claims on the United States, shows how misleading it can be to look only at the 1980s: the surge of portfolio investment in the 1980s masked the trend toward increasing FDI as opposed to portfolio investment that marked the 1970s. It is difficult to see how to reconcile the kind of large shifts seen here with a view that FDI is closely tied to capital inflows in general.

Another piece of evidence in favor of an industrial-organization explanation is the large variance of foreign control across sectors of the US economy. Table 2.1 shows how the share of gross product originating from foreign firms varied widely

Table 2.1 Share of gross product controlled by foreign firms in the United States, by industry, 1986 (percentages)

Industry	Share
Mining	13.4
Petroleum	18.7
Manufacturing	8.0
Food and kindred products	9.4
Chemicals and allied products	32.8
Primary metals	12.2
Fabricated metal products	4.6
Nonelectrical machinery	5.4
Electric and electronic equipment	9.1
Textile products and apparel	2.3
Lumber, wood, furniture, fixtures	1.4
Paper and allied products	5.8
Printing and publishing	6.3
Rubber and plastic products	2.5
Stone, clay, and glass products	15.2
Transportation equipment	10.3
Instruments	5.0
Other manufactured goods	2.6
Wholesale trade	6.5
Retail trade	2.8
Finance, insurance, and real estate[a]	2.5

a. Excluding banking.

Source: Bureau of Economic Analysis, "Foreign Direct Investment in the United States: Gross Product of Nonbank U.S. Affiliates of Foreign Companies, 1977–1986," and "National Income and Product Accounts," *Survey of Current Business* 67 (July 1987).

across sectors in 1986. It is hard to see why there should be such large variances if direct investment were simply a by-product of differences in the cost of capital.

Finally, the composition of FDI by nationality of owner is a key piece of evidence in favor of industrial-organization rather than cost-of-capital explanations of FDI. We have already noted that although Japan has been the principal exporter of capital in the world economy in the 1980s, it has accounted for only a small share of the increased foreign presence in the United States. Table 2.2 makes the point more generally, by showing the percentage distribution of FDI by country of parent. What is striking is not only that the United Kingdom, which has not been a large net exporter of capital to the United States in this century, remains the largest foreign direct investor, but also that its share has been sharply increasing. In other words, even though the United Kingdom has not been running current surpluses

Table 2.2 Distribution of foreign direct investment in the United States by country of owner, 1980–1988 (percentages of total FDI stock)

Country	1980	1981	1982	1983	1984	1985	1986	1987	1988
United Kingdom	16.6	17.2	23.0	24.0	23.3	23.9	25.4	29.3	31.0
Netherlands	25.0	24.9	21.0	21.3	20.5	19.7	18.5	18.1	14.9
Japan	6.2	7.1	7.8	8.2	9.7	10.4	12.2	12.9	16.2
Canada	14.4	11.0	9.3	8.2	9.3	9.1	9.2	8.8	8.3

Sources: For 1980–86, Bureau of Economic Analysis, "Foreign Direct Investment in the United States: Detail for Position and Balance of Payments Flows," *Survey of Current Business* (August, various years); for 1987 and 1988, Bureau of Economic Analysis, "Growth in Foreign Direct Investment in the United States Outpaced That of U.S. Direct Investment Abroad in 1988," US Department of Commerce news release (BEA 89–31), 29 June 1989, table 1.

corresponding to the US external deficits, it has been increasing its FDI in the United States at a rate faster than the general increase.

What explanation of the growth in FDI is suggested by this evidence? Twenty years ago, US–based firms had significant advantages over firms from other countries in terms of technology and management skills. These advantages were reflected in a variety of ways: in the United States' position at the top of the product life cycle, in the large US trade surplus in high-technology products, and in the ability of US firms to pay much higher wages than firms elsewhere. This superiority also meant that US–based firms, besides often having an advantage over foreign rivals even in producing abroad, almost always had such an advantage at home. The result was that there was little direct investment by foreigners in the United States.

What has happened over the past two decades is an erosion of that US superiority on all fronts. The reasons for that erosion are the subject of intense debate, but the fact of erosion is not. As US economic leadership has diminished, US margins in productivity have narrowed, the US position as the innovating country in the product life cycle has become ambiguous, and the United States has become almost as much an importer as an exporter of high-technology goods. It is not surprising in this context that the one-sided relationship between the United States and multinational enterprises should also have changed; instead of US firms having a uniform advantage, there are now many areas in which foreign-based firms have technological or managerial advantages that enable them to produce more effectively even in the United States.

In other words, we regard the data as most consistent with the view that growing inward FDI in the United States is a part of the general decline of US economic preeminence rather than a by-product of the trade deficits of the 1980s. It is important to be careful in interpreting this view: although FDI here is a symptom of relative US decline, it need not be viewed as a cause. Indeed, as we argue in Chapter 3, a good case can be made that inward FDI will help to limit that decline. This explanation of the causes of FDI does not carry with it any immediate policy implications.

The Role of Financial Markets

We have argued that the rising share of foreign firms in US production may be attributed primarily to shifts in international technology and comparative advantage, and the resulting consequences to long-term corporate strategies and advantages, rather than to the differences in costs and returns that have made the United States an aggregate capital importer in the 1980s. However, popular discussion of FDI—notably the critical discussions by Rohatyn (1989), among others—has focused attention on the role of financial developments. In particular, the combination of a dollar that is low by historical standards and a strong Japanese stock market has been alleged to be causing a "fire sale" of US assets to foreign firms.

This argument needs careful discussion. The assertion that the United States is impoverishing itself by selling assets off cheaply is dealt with at some length in our discussion of the welfare effects of FDI in Chapter 3. For now let us simply focus on the question of whether the weak dollar, the strong Japanese stock market, or both can reasonably be invoked as major causes of rising FDI.

There is an evident correlation between recent changes in FDI flows into the United States and the movements of the dollar. During the weak-dollar period of the late 1970s and early 1980s there was a first surge of direct investment into the United States. This surge then trailed off as the dollar rose, to be followed by the current surge that began in late 1986 as the dollar fell. The weakness of the dollar is commonly cited in the business press as a motive for FDI.

At first sight it seems obvious that the weak dollar makes producing in the United States more attractive, and thus makes acquisition or establishment of new facilities in the United States more attractive as well. However, this proposition neglects the point that the FDI decision always depends on a *comparative* assessment: is this factory worth more to a foreign firm than to a domestic one? A fall in the dollar that raises the expected returns to a US owner by the same amount that it raises the returns to a foreign owner should not lead to net purchases by foreigners.

One must also ask, If US real assets in general have become more attractive to foreign investors, why did the dollar fall? The fall in the dollar must reflect some general downward revision of opinions about the eventual value of claims on the United States. If everyone knew that US assets were undervalued, they would not be so cheap.

To establish a link between a weak dollar and increased FDI, then, it is necessary to establish some reason for a differential effect of the dollar's fall on the attractiveness of assets to foreign and domestic firms. There are several possible arguments, which we summarize briefly.

One argument places the emphasis on the changing composition of US output associated with the dollar's decline. That decline, to the extent that it affects US competitiveness, is bringing about a shift in US output from nontraded sectors like services and retail trade toward tradeable sectors like manufacturing. As we have already noted, however, FDI in the United States is strongly concentrated in tradeable sectors, presumably because the strategic advantages that make an enterprise in the United States worth more to a foreign firm are much more likely to occur in industries engaged in tradeable production. In particular, half of FDI in the United States is in manufacturing, which accounts for only 20 percent of GNP, and the dollar's decline has been associated with a revival of US manufacturing output and investment.

We can now see how a declining dollar could be associated with a rise in the role of FDI: as the economy shifts from production of nontraded to traded goods, it also shifts from activities in which foreign-based multinationals have little role to areas in which they have a much larger role. Consider the following extreme numerical example. Suppose that all foreign subsidiaries are in the tradeable sector, which we take initially to represent 20 percent of GNP. Suppose also that the US current account deficit were to decline by 3 percent of GNP, with all of the improvement taking place through increased tradeable production. Then, even with a constant foreign share of the tradeable sector we would see a 15 percent rise in foreign control of the US economy.

In the case of the United States, where there is a long-run trend toward a rising share of foreign control, changes in the exchange rate may also have an important effect on the timing of increases in foreign ownership. Suppose that foreign firms have a greater advantage over US firms in newly constructed capacity than in existing capacity. Then in an industry in which foreign firms have a potential advantage, this advantage is likely to go unrealized if there is little capacity expansion. Thus, when the dollar was strong and US tradeable industries were static or shrinking, foreign shares were stagnant. Once it became profitable to build new capacity in tradeable industries, however, the foreign share surged back to its long-run upward trend.

However, given the crucial role played by acquisitions in the growth of foreign control in the United States, this cannot be the full story. A second explanation, emphasized by Froot and Stein (1989), stresses valuation effects. The rise of foreign currencies against the dollar raises the book value of foreign firms compared to US firms. To the extent that firms are capital-constrained, with their potential borrowing limited by their debt-equity ratios, this rise increases the purchasing power of foreign firms; this may lead a foreign firm to outbid a domestic firm in an acquisition contest even when the expected present value of the target is the same in either firm's hands. A variant on the Froot-Stein explanation would emphasize the increased opportunities for managerial empire building that would result from the decline of the dollar. A weak dollar may make it easier for the executives of foreign-owned companies to expand their firms even when such expansion is contrary to the interests of their original stockholders.

A third explanation is one that allows for some misplaced investor concreteness. Foreign investors may focus on the fact that US real assets appear cheap compared with physically equivalent assets abroad and neglect the question of whether the economic returns are really equivalent.

Whatever the role of the dollar in triggering booms and slumps in FDI, it should be borne in mind that these fluctuations take place around a long-term rising trend. The timing of surges in FDI may be attributable at least in part to movements in the dollar, but the decline in the dollar cannot explain the long-run upward trend in foreign control that has continued since the mid-1970s.

The role of stock market divergences is more difficult to assess, partly because the financial events themselves are so hard to understand. What, for example, does the incredible surge of Japanese stock prices in recent years mean?

We can at least offer a hypothetical scenario. Suppose that for some reason there is an irrational bubble that causes Japanese stocks to rise to unprecedented heights. If Japanese firms realize that this is a bubble, and if they are willing to issue new equity to take advantage of the high stock prices, then this will in effect lower their firm-specific costs of capital and allow them to invest abroad even when their expected returns are lower than those of domestic firms. In effect, those who buy Japanese stocks would be subsidizing the acquisition of US assets by Japanese firms.

A major question, obviously, is who pays the subsidy. As long as the Japanese boom is a domestic affair, the answer is the Japanese themselves. Only to the extent that US residents buy into overpriced Japanese stocks can we say that the United States is giving up its own assets cheaply.

Taxation

The 1980s have been marked by two major changes in US tax policy: the tax cuts of 1981 and the tax reform of 1986. Although it is natural to suppose that these tax changes should have had an important effect on FDI in the United States, it is important to be careful in assessing the impact of taxation. FDI is primarily about control rather than movement of capital. Thus, we need to ask how the tax laws affect the tax burdens on US activities owned by foreign corporations differently from those on operations owned domestically. An interesting argument, first advanced by Scholes and Wolfson (1988), suggests how changes in the tax law may have contributed to the timing of surges and slumps in FDI.

Of the four countries with the largest shares of FDI in the United States, the Netherlands and Canada have "territorial" corporate taxation, which does not attempt to tax the income of subsidiaries abroad, whereas the United Kingdom and Japan have "worldwide" systems that tax subsidiaries but grant a tax credit for taxes paid to host-country governments. Changes in taxation should in principle have a major impact on the investment decisions of firms based in countries with a tax credit system.

Abstracting from the immensely complicated details, a worldwide system works as follows. Subsidiaries of foreign firms pay corporate taxes to the US government just as if they were domestic firms. However, when they repatriate income to their parent company, they are liable to taxation at the home-country rate, with a credit for any taxes paid to the US government.

If both the US and the foreign governments levied straightforward corporate taxes at the same rate, this system would be neutral in its effect on the ownership of productive assets. A foreign-owned enterprise in the United States would pay normal US taxes; these would then give it a tax credit exactly equal to the tax liability to the home-country government, so that no taxes would be paid abroad. Other things equal, a shift from domestic to foreign ownership would have no effect either on total tax liability or on the distribution of revenues between the US and other governments.

The neutrality of taxation for FDI breaks down, sometimes in surprising ways, when corporate tax regimes differ across countries. Consider, for example, the effect of a reduction in the US corporate tax rate that is not matched by tax cuts abroad. One might expect that this would encourage foreign investment in the US generally, and that FDI would rise along with the rest. In fact, however, such a cut, while encouraging portfolio investment in the United States, would put foreign-owned firms at a disadvantage relative to domestically owned firms. The domestically owned firms would receive a tax reduction by the full amount of the tax cut. Foreign subsidiaries, however, would find their tax credit reduced, and thus their lower US tax liability would be offset by an increased liability to the home-country government. Other things equal, then, reducing corporate tax rates in the United States would make foreign control of US firms less attractive.

In the 1980s US corporate tax policy shifted twice. In the early 1980s corporate taxation was cut sharply, notably by the introduction of accelerated depreciation. The tax advantages of accelerated depreciation were valuable to US–owned corporations but could have been worth much less to foreign-owned firms, since they were offset by reduced domestic tax credits. Thus, the tax regime for much of the 1980s acted as a substantial disincentive to FDI in the

United States from some countries. Conversely, the 1986 tax reform eliminated the special investment incentives and thus the bias against foreign ownership.

In practice, the story is not quite so clear-cut, because of the combined effects of deferral of taxation and mixing of tax credits. Consider a UK firm with a US subsidiary, in a situation in which the United Kingdom has a higher effective corporate tax rate than the United States. The analysis above suggests that a reduction in the US corporate tax rate would provide this firm with no advantages. The UK firm, however, pays taxes only when earnings are repatriated; it therefore has an incentive to defer repatriation, allowing its profits to be taxed at the lower US rate in the meantime; thus, the present value of its tax liability will fall if the US tax rate falls. Also, the firm may be in an excess tax credit position, with no offset to changes in US tax collection at the margin, even though the US tax rate is lower than that in the United Kingdom. This could happen if the firm has other subsidiaries in countries with still higher tax rates, such as Germany, and must mix the tax credits from these subsidiaries with the credits from US subsidiaries.

Perhaps because of these complications, cross-sectional evidence does not agree too well with the view that changes in taxation have been of decisive importance for the observed shifts in FDI since 1980. Tax considerations alone would have led one to expect a decline in the relative share of Japan and the United Kingdom and a rise in the relative share of Canada and the Netherlands from 1981 to 1986, followed by a reversal; in fact, no such clear pattern is visible. More elaborate investigation by Slemrod (1989) also fails to show a strong tax effect on FDI. Nonetheless, the potentially important role of taxation in determining FDI cannot be dismissed.

Protection

Case studies of decisions by foreign firms to invest in the United States, especially in manufacturing, often give a key role to actual or possible protectionist measures by the United States. Thus, protection needs to be considered in any explanation of the rise of foreign firms in the United States. As in the case of taxation, however, it is important to be careful in defining the question. We need to ask not whether protection makes it more attractive for a foreign firm to produce in the United States, but whether it makes production by foreign-owned firms more attractive relative to production by domestic firms.

Consider the effects of a tariff or import quota imposed on some industry. By protecting the industry, the United States can induce a shift of production from foreign locations to domestic. The domestic production could, however, be undertaken by domestic firms—after all, US import quotas on cheese and sugar have not led to the wholesale establishment of foreign-owned dairies and sugar plantations in the United States. To explain why foreign firms establish or expand their US subsidiaries, it is necessary to start with some explanation of why the foreign firms have an advantage over domestic ones to begin with. This firm-specific advantage, rather than the protection, should be regarded as the underlying source of the FDI.

There is nonetheless a sense in which it is probably true that protection has tended to increase the extent of foreign control in the US economy, but the argument is more subtle than is usually appreciated. It is that there is a bias in protection: an industry that appeals for protection is especially likely to be one in which foreign firms have some kind of special advantage. (This is apparent in the case of automobiles and that of color televisions, discussed in the next section.) Thus, protectionism in effect biases the US economy toward producing those goods that foreign firms can produce better than domestic firms. An analogy with developing countries may be useful. Protectionism in these countries has often promoted FDI because it pushes their economies into activities in which they do not have comparative advantage, and as a result domestic firms have little aptitude; it is this shift in the mix of production rather than the incentives offered by protection per se that explain the association of protectionism and FDI.

Protectionism, then, plays a key role in the specifics of FDI in some important industries and has had some effect in increasing the overall foreign share in the US economy, but it is not a fundamental explanation of the rising trend.

Three Case Histories

Color Televisions

The case of color television production in the United States provides a useful illustration of the forces underlying FDI. In many respects this industry is both an early and an extreme example of the role of foreign firms in the United States. Although the United States imports many color televisions, there is still a significant amount of domestic production: more than half of the color sets sold in the United States are at least assembled in the United States. The domestic industry is, however, for the most part foreign controlled. Large-scale acquisition and establishment of US subsidiaries by foreign firms began in the late 1970s; since the sale of General Electric's television production operations to Thomson, a French group, in 1987, the industry has contained only one major US–based firm, Zenith.

The basic story of color television production is quite simple: foreign producers, especially the Japanese, had developed by the mid-1970s both a better design and a better production system than their US rivals. When US firms appealed for and received protection, in the form of a voluntary export restraint (VER) agreement, the foreign firms moved to establish production facilities in the United States. The firm-specific assets that had enabled the foreign firms to outperform US firms proved both transferable and appropriable, so that US firms found themselves crowded out despite protection.

The advantage established by Japanese firms in color televisions was of a kind that has become depressingly familiar. Japanese televisions were designed with many fewer parts than US sets, allowing greater efficiency and reliability, both as a direct result of simplicity and because the simpler design lent itself better to automation. Coupled with this design advantage was an emphasis on quality control that both greatly reduced the need for testing and repair before sale and delivered much more reliable sets to consumers. Matsushita's acquisition of a Motorola factory in Illinois exemplifies the strong Japanese advantage. After the acquisition, productivity increased by 30 percent, and defects were cut to a small fraction of former levels (Lewis 1982).

Ironically, US firms, unable to match Japanese productivity or quality, responded by attempting to compete on the basis of labor costs, shifting to heavy sourcing from developing countries. The result was that, in terms of location of production for the US market, Japanese firms became more American than US firms. In 1987 Japanese firms produced 6 million color televisions in the United States, whereas only 1.4 million were imported from Japan (although a much higher share of components came from Japan). Meanwhile, Zenith maintained only one television and one picture-tube plant in the United States; the bulk of Zenith's television manufacturing is now located in Mexico.

This reversal of roles is interesting for our discussion of the economic consequences of FDI in Chapter 3. The important point here is that the advantage of Japanese producers, it is clear, came from superior technology and management techniques that proved transferable to US production. The shift from US to foreign control in this industry had nothing to do with inflow of capital as such.

Automobiles

The growing Japanese presence in the US auto industry has attracted widespread attention. Honda began producing automobiles in the United States in 1982 and has been followed by five other Japanese manufacturers. Most estimates suggest that by the early 1990s Japanese-affiliated plants will produce at least 20 percent of the output of cars and trucks in the United States, with a somewhat smaller share of value added because of a lower domestic content in the Japanese product.

In broad outline, there are strong resemblances between this case and that of color televisions. As in the television case, the initial Japanese move to US production was prompted by a VER agreement. This incentive was reinforced by the rise in value of the yen against the dollar after 1985. However, these incentives to increase production in the United States could have been met by expanded production by US firms, and indeed have been to some extent. The reason why Japanese rather than US firms have been adding US capacity lies in the firm-specific advantages of the Japanese: the now-familiar but still hard-to-emulate differences in organization that make not only plants in Japan but also Japanese-owned plants in the United States more productive than those owned by US firms.

The automotive sector also provides a useful case study of the differences in behavior between foreign and domestic firms, as discussed in Chapter 3.

Banking

As we noted in Chapter 1, FDI in the US banking sector differs from FDI in other sectors on a number of measures. The foreign presence in this industry, as measured by the share of total US banking assets under foreign control, is much greater than in other sectors, and the Japanese presence within this sector is much larger. Industrial-organization-based theories of FDI do not seem as robust in this sector as in, for example, manufacturing.

One explanation often given for the large foreign presence in banking is that banks follow their customers abroad. For example, if manufacturing companies headquartered in Japan create subsidiaries in the United States, the Japanese banks with which these companies have their principal relations will establish US operations primarily to service the banking needs of these subsidiaries. But if this were the only explanation of the foreign presence in banking, one might expect US banking assets under Japanese control to be substantially less than those under British control and about equal to those under Dutch control. As we saw in Chapter 1, however, the share of US banking assets under Japanese control is greater than the combined shares for all other countries. To explain the extent of foreign control of US banking assets, one must account for the larger-than-expected Japanese presence.

Various explanations have been advanced to explain this presence. One explanation invokes the need for Japanese banks to create US operations in order to participate in the market for dollar-denominated bankers' acceptances to finance oil imports. Another explanation sees the large Japanese banking presence as a means to help intermediate Japan's current account surpluses. These surpluses in turn are in large part accounted for by Japan's bilateral trade surplus with the United States. Hence, unlike for other forms of direct participation by foreign investors in the US economy, for Japanese banking there might be a strong direct link with the US current account deficit. Thus, unlike for other sectors, the Japanese presence in banking might be better explained by financial-market considerations than by industrial-organization considerations.

It is widely claimed that Japanese banks have a cost of capital lower than that of their non-Japanese competitors and that this allows them to practice predatory pricing to increase market share. The high price-earnings ratios of Japanese banks relative to US banks lend some support to this claim. However, this argument is subject to the same criticisms as the "fire sale" explanation of Japanese FDI in general (discussed elsewhere in this chapter). Still another explanation of the strong presence of Japanese banks in foreign markets sees it as a means to circumvent home-market banking regulations and as a reflection of the propensity of these banks to follow one another into new activities (Terrell et al. 1989). These arguments may have some validity, but at present the phenomenon remains something of a mystery.

What about the non-Japanese foreign presence in the banking sector? As table 1.7 showed, the nationals of no country other than Japan hold a particularly large share of US banking assets. While it is possible that financial-market considerations are part of the story for these other foreign banks as well, the industrial-organization explanation seems to be equally plausible. That is, the non-Japanese foreign banks might be present in the United States simply to service the needs of US subsidiaries of nonbanking firms headquartered in their home countries.

The Outlook for FDI

The United States has gone in the course of a decade from having a very small foreign economic presence to the point where FDI in the United States, as measured by book value, now exceeds US direct investment abroad. In 1980 US inward FDI stood at $83.0 billion and outward FDI at $220.2 billion; by mid-1989 FDI in the United States had grown to an estimated $360.3 billion whereas American FDI abroad amounted to only an estimated $337.8 billion. The natural question is how far this trend will go: how much of the US economy will end up being controlled by foreign-based firms?

Much popular discussion poses this as a question about the dependence of the United States on foreign capital inflows, putting the question in terms of how fast the United States can bring its current account into balance. We have argued, however, that the rise in FDI has little to do with capital inflows; the United States could continue to import capital without further expansion of foreign firms, or (more likely) it could bring its current account into balance and still find that foreign firms continue to expand, as they did during the 1970s.

We argue that the rise of inward FDI is part of a process by which the United States is becoming a "normal" country in which multinational firms play about the same role as in other industrial countries. There is no longer a presumption that multinationals are headquartered in the United States. This suggests that FDI will not grow indefinitely, but rather that it will approach a natural limit when foreign firms have expanded into all those sectors in which their specific advantages outweigh the "home-court" advantage of US firms.

A useful model for the United States may be the European countries. Foreign firms appear to have about twice as large a role in the major European nations as in the United States. This role appears to have stabilized in spite of growing international integration on other fronts, suggesting that FDI has reached a sort of natural limit in Europe. It is thus reasonable to suppose that something similar may happen in the United States. Part of FDI in Europe, moreover, represents intra-European holdings that would be counted as domestic in the United States. We would therefore expect the foreign role in the United States to settle eventually at a level somewhat lower than that in Europe.

It seems reasonable, then, to suppose that the European experience provides an upper bound for the extent of possible foreign control of the US economy at something less than twice the current level. Despite the fears raised in Europe in the 1960s, Europe does not exactly look like a colonized economy; in particular, the substantial foreign share in the European economy does not prevent Europe from being in turn a substantial direct investor abroad.

Conclusions

The composition and history of growth in FDI in the United States seem inconsistent with a view that such investment is driven by international differences in the cost of capital. Instead, the growth of inward FDI seems best viewed as part of the general decline in US technological and managerial superiority. This means, in particular, that growing foreign investment in the United States has little to do with the US trade deficit and the resulting growth in aggregate foreign claims.

The recent stress on the role of a low dollar and high stock prices in Japan as explanations of rising FDI may contain a grain of truth, in that each could explain some increase in the foreign presence. However, the potential role for these explanations is limited, and the major explanation of the rising foreign presence must lie elsewhere.

Changes in taxation may well have played an important role in determining the timing of FDI in the United States. The system of US corporate taxation from 1981 to 1986 probably discouraged inward FDI, temporarily delaying the underlying upward trend.

3

Economic Impact

The Gains From FDI

Much of the recent discussion of rising foreign direct investment in the United States has focused on the possible risks and costs. It seems appropriate as a starting point, however, to discuss the potential benefits. After all, direct investment is a form of international integration, and as with more conventional forms of integration such as trade in goods and services or portfolio investment, we may take as a first presumption that it yields gains in efficiency. Only once we have thought about these gains does it make sense to turn to the potential costs.

Broadly, we may divide the potential gains from FDI into two categories. First are the conventional gains from integration: to the extent that FDI in effect facilitates trade in goods and services, it increases the conventional benefits that we normally associate with such trade. Second are the external economies: the benefits that may result from FDI but are not part of the motivation of the firms that engage in it.

Benefits From Increased Integration

The standard analysis of the gains from international trade recognizes three sources for such gains. The first is comparative advantage: countries are different, and trade enables them to specialize and benefit from their differences. The second is increasing returns to scale: trade allows each country to produce a narrower range of goods than it otherwise would, and thereby to achieve a larger and more efficient scale of production. The third is increased competition: trade effectively widens the scope of competition, reducing monopoly power.

In the industrial-organization view of FDI that we have argued is the principal explanation of the growth of FDI in the United States, a multinational firm may be thought of as a facilitating device for trade in goods, services, and knowledge. In some cases transactions costs may be reduced when international trade takes the form of intrafirm trade rather than arm's-length transactions between unrelated parties; in some cases services, such as the coordination provided by the headquarters, may be difficult to trade on any market but can effectively be exchanged internationally under the umbrella of a multinational firm. Perhaps the classic example of how a multinational can facilitate trade is the case of trade in knowledge; given the well-known problems of markets in information, a firm may not be able to appropriate the benefits of its own research and development (R&D) via patents or licensing. Producing the relevant goods itself may then allow *de facto* trade in the results of R&D, providing the inducement to engage in the activity.

To the extent that FDI facilitates trade in goods, services, and knowledge, it magnifies the gains from trade. Countries will be able to specialize more effectively—in the production of intangibles such as knowledge as well as tangible goods—and thus to benefit from both comparative advantage and economies of scale. At the same time competition will be increased.

How large are these gains? Unfortunately, there does not seem to be any way to get even an order-of-magnitude estimate. In 1986, 21 percent of US exports were sold and 34 percent of US imports were purchased by US affiliates of foreign firms. Slightly less than half of the exports of these US affiliates were to their foreign parent groups, whereas slightly more than three-quarters of the affiliates' imports were from the foreign parents. However, we do not know how much more costly it would have been to conduct these transactions through other mechanisms. Furthermore, many of the gains from FDI presumably take place through exchanges of intangibles, such as knowledge. And in any case, gains from rationalization and increased competition may exceed the direct reduction in the cost of transacting.

The bottom line is that FDI may be expected to bring gains from integration that are qualitatively similar to the conventional gains from trade, but the magnitude of these gains is anyone's guess.

External Benefits

Advocates of more liberal treatment of FDI in developing countries typically argue that such investment brings benefits over and above the usual gains from trade, because of valuable spillovers to the domestic economy. The benefits usually cited are the introduction of technology that can be emulated by other firms and the training of workers who may then transfer their skills elsewhere. In each case the point is that the foreign firm is not able fully to appropriate the benefits of its activities.

Exactly the same arguments can be made for foreign firms in the United States. To the extent that foreign firms introduce new technology and this technology diffuses to other parts of the US economy, FDI brings benefits over and above the usual gains from integration. (Technology here is defined broadly, to include not only science- and engineering-based production innovations but also management methods.) Thus, if US firms learn about just-in-time inventory methods or even about the benefits of listening to their workers by observing US affiliates of Japanese firms, they will be deriving a benefit that magnifies the US gains from FDI. Similarly, if US workers receive training from affiliates of foreign firms and then bring those skills to new jobs elsewhere, they will be deriving benefits from FDI over and above the gains from increased international exchange.

These external benefits from FDI are even less measurable than the gains from integration. It is important, however, to bear them in mind as a corrective. In discussion of FDI there is a tendency to use any departure from perfect markets as a debating point against FDI—that is, to assume that any external effects are likely to represent costs that must be set against the more conventional benefits. In fact, *a priori* market failures are as likely to lead to too little as to too much FDI, and it is possible to argue at least as strongly for hidden benefits from FDI as for hidden costs.

The Potential Costs of FDI

Most discussion of FDI has been motivated by the fear that such investment carries costs for the United States. A good deal of this fear is of risks to sovereignty or national security. However, we postpone discussion of these issues until Chapters 4 and 5 in order to focus first on the more purely economic issues.

We should also note that our discussion, in focusing on the effects of inward FDI, neglects concerns about the general role of multinational firms, domestic as well as foreign, in the US economy. For example, it is sometimes alleged that multinationals, by facilitating international capital movements, weaken the bargaining power of US labor in general. There is a huge literature (although no consensus) on these issues; we choose here to limit our focus to those issues that arise specifically from the role of FDI in the United States.

Economic arguments against FDI may be arrayed on a scale of increasing sophistication. At the crudest level, charges are made that FDI will cost jobs or worsen the trade deficit. More sophisticated arguments are that FDI will bias US production and employment toward inappropriate activities, that externality-generating activities such as R&D will be shifted abroad, or that openness of the United States to FDI puts domestic firms at a strategic disadvantage. We will consider some evidence that bears on these concerns shortly; however, as an initial step we examine the underlying logic.

Employment Effects

Much of the popular debate over the economic effects of FDI has focused on its alleged impact on employment and, in what is usually seen as a related issue, the US trade balance. On one side, enthusiastic advocates of inward FDI point to the large number of employees hired by foreign-owned firms and argue that this represents substantial job creation. On the other side, critics argue that foreign owners tend to obtain more of their production inputs from abroad than do US owners, and that the resulting reduced demand for the products of domestic suppliers both costs the United States jobs and worsens the US trade balance. Responding to this debate, many studies of FDI have tried to measure the direct and indirect effects of such investment on employment. For example, the well-received recent study by Glickman and Woodward (1989) has as one of its central arguments a debunking of claims of significant job creation by foreign investors; a recent US General Accounting Office study of foreign investment in the automobile industry (1988) also essentially concerns itself with employment impacts.

We will not follow this route, because we regard an emphasis on job creation as fundamentally mistaken. The dominance of this issue in public discussion of FDI represents a misunderstanding of the nature of the problem. FDI almost surely has very little net effect on overall employment in the United States; this conclusion has nothing to do with the results of calculations of net job effects at the industry level, but rests on the macroeconomic point that employment in the United States is essentially determined by supply, not demand, except in the very short run. This does not mean that there is no potential problem arising from a high propensity of foreign-owned firms to source abroad. The problem, however, concerns the impact of FDI on the long-term value of the dollar and hence on the US terms of trade, rather than the impact on employment.

In the US economy of the late 20th century, creating demand for goods and services is not a problem, because of the active role of the Federal Reserve. Faced with an incipient shortfall of demand, the Federal Reserve can easily cut interest rates, thus offsetting the fall in demand and maintaining the level of employment. The aftermath of the stock market crash in October 1987 demonstrated this role clearly: the Federal Reserve's willingness to offset the crash by reducing interest rates not only averted a major recession but actually kept unemployment on its downward trend.

What constrains the Federal Reserve from driving unemployment down to even lower levels is not any difficulty in creating demand but fear of inflation. It is widely accepted among economists that the US economy has a so-called nonaccelerating-inflation rate of unemployment (NAIRU) below which the unemployment rate cannot be driven without causing inflation to spiral upward; this rate is generally estimated to lie in the 5 to 6 percent range. The essential determinant of the unemployment rate is therefore not the level of demand—this is not a given, but a policy variable that the Federal Reserve controls—but the NAIRU, which reflects the structure of the labor market. Unless it affects the NAIRU, FDI will have essentially no effect on employment.

Suppose, for example, that a wave of FDI into the United States turned out to have a substantial immediate positive effect on demand for US workers. The normal response of the Federal Reserve would be to tighten monetary policy to avoid accelerating inflation, so that any job gains resulting from the investment would be offset by job losses elsewhere. Conversely, a wave of investment that had a negative impact on the demand for labor would be met by looser monetary policy and thus be offset by job gains elsewhere.

The main way in which FDI could affect the NAIRU would be if the shifts in employment associated with foreign investment either aggravated or diminished the mismatch between workers and jobs that is one reason the NAIRU is as high as it is. For example, suppose that workers laid off by foreign firms were typically either in already depressed regions or in skill categories of which there is an excess supply. Then the NAIRU might increase as a result of increased foreign ownership. There is also evidently a converse case in which foreign firms effectively lower the NAIRU. The point is that such effects, whatever their direction, are certain to be much smaller than the overall job creation or displacement numbers calculated when looking at the demand side and will generally be unrelated to the typical measures of net employment impact.

This does not mean that studies of the impact of FDI on employment in particular industries are of no interest. For example, it is clearly of considerable interest to learn what the effect of Japanese direct investment will be on employment in the US auto industry. (Even this is hard to determine, since it is unclear how much of the new Japanese production substitutes for imports and how much for production by domestic firms; see the discussion of trade in the next section.) However, this effect should not be construed as a measure of the effect of this Japanese investment on US employment as a whole, nor should we imagine that the overall effect of all FDI could be estimated by adding up estimates from a series of industry studies. *The net impact of FDI on US employment is approximately zero*, and the truth of this assertion has nothing to do with job gains and losses estimated at the industry level.

Trade Balance Effects

Related to the question of the employment effects of foreign ownership is that of trade balance effects. It is often alleged that foreign-owned firms have a higher propensity to source abroad than do their domestically owned counterparts and that, as a result, increasing foreign ownership worsens the US trade deficit.

In part this issue can be addressed in the same way as the employment issue, by pointing out that macroeconomics, not microeconomics, determines the trade balance. By definition, the US current account deficit is equal to the difference between domestic investment and domestic saving; thus, the deficit fundamentally reflects our low level of national saving. Microeconomic events, including changes in import propensities, cannot affect the trade balance unless they somehow affect savings or investment demand.

The principal mechanism through which the savings-investment identity is reconciled with microeconomic decisions about trade is the exchange rate. Suppose that there were widespread foreign takeovers of US businesses, and that the foreign owners exhibited a much higher propensity to import than US firms. Unless the foreign acquisitions also somehow reduced US savings or increased US real investment, the higher import propensity would be offset by a fall in the value of the dollar that would encourage exports, discourage imports, and leave the overall US trade balance (although not the trade balance in particular industries) unchanged.

Because of the macroeconomic determination of the balance of payments, then, even systematic differences in the trading behavior of domestic and foreign firms will not in general be reflected in the overall US trade balance. However, this does not mean that a high propensity to import on the part of foreign-owned firms is not a cause for concern. The reason for concern is that the offset to such a propensity is a weaker dollar, and the need for a persistently weaker dollar would itself represent a cost to the US economy.

For this reason the trade behavior of foreign-owned firms is an important consideration in assessing the costs and benefits of FDI. As we will see, the available data do indeed suggest that foreign-owned firms have a substantially stronger tendency to source abroad than do domestic firms; thus, there is an argument that an adverse trade impact from inward FDI exists, on the grounds that a growing share of foreign ownership implies the need for a weaker dollar.

Valid as this argument may be, it must be treated carefully. First, we need to note that even where foreign firms appear to have a higher import propensity than domestic firms, their expansion need not have a negative effect on the trade balance at any given exchange rate. Those direct investments that are essentially creations of marketing arms—which, as we will see, account for most of the imports by US affiliates of foreign firms—should not be considered as shifting demand away from US suppliers. Also, while greenfield plants that foreign firms add to an industry's capacity may not purchase as much from domestic suppliers as do existing facilities, they may displace imports rather than domestic production and thus reduce overall imports in the industry. For example, a US General Accounting Office study of Japanese investment in the automobile industry concludes that, in spite of a higher propensity on the part of Japanese automobile plants to import components, such investment will actually reduce imports if as much as 40 percent of the Japanese production displaces imports of finished cars instead of sales by US manufacturers (US General Accounting Office 1988).

Second, there is a factual question: do affiliates of foreign firms actually have a higher propensity to import than domestic firms in the same line of business? As we will see later in this chapter, they do appear to have a higher import propensity, but some of this may reflect not so much a difference in behavior as a bias in the type of activity in which foreign firms engage.

Finally, there is the question of magnitudes: to what extent does growing foreign ownership weaken the dollar? We present some estimates later in this chapter that suggest that even on the most pessimistic assumptions the impact of foreign ownership on the equilibrium value of the dollar is quite small.

The assertion that direct effects of FDI on jobs and trade are not important will probably not pacify the political process—we will certainly want to look at what these effects are likely to be. It is worth emphasizing, however, that in an assessment of the true costs and benefits of FDI in the United States an evaluation of direct impacts on economy-wide employment and trade is simply not an important part of the story.

In drawing these conclusions, we differ from a number of other studies, notably Hufbauer and Adler (1968) and Bergsten, Horst, and Moran (1978), who looked at the effects of US *outward* FDI on US employment and the US balance of payments, as well as Glickman and Woodward (1989), who looked at the effects of inward FDI on these same aggregates. The major difference between these studies and the present one is that we are implicitly considering these effects in a context of general equilibrium, whereas they considered them in a context of partial equilibrium. Under partial-equilibrium analysis, one assumes that nothing changes except the independent and the dependent variables immediately under consideration. (Here, the independent variable is the stock of FDI, and the dependent variables are levels of employment and balance of payments variables.) The estimates thus represent an intermediate result: a calculation of changes in the dependent variables under an assumption that these changes do not induce still further changes that ultimately feed back to affect these variables. But further changes will indeed occur. Thus, under general-equilibrium analysis, one assumes that all economic variables simultaneously are affected by the change in the independent variable, and one seeks to determine the ultimate change in the relevant dependent variables. This ultimate change, it should be clear, is what is relevant for policy analysis purposes.

Quality of Employment

We have seen that the argument that FDI can reduce employment or persistently worsen the trade deficit does not make much sense. A different and potentially more valid argument is that FDI could shift the quality of employment in an unfavorable way, reducing the number of "good jobs" and replacing them with "bad jobs."

The idea of good versus bad jobs is one that needs some discussion. In an efficient labor market there would be no such distinction. Skilled workers would be paid more than unskilled, but this would simply reflect their differences in human capital—good workers versus bad workers, not good jobs versus bad jobs. Other things equal, a worker would be paid the same in any sector or activity.

In reality, there are substantial differences across sectors in the wages paid to seemingly equivalent workers. Recent work in labor economics (e.g., Shapiro and Stiglitz 1984) has suggested that there may be systematic market failures leading to wage differentials between sectors. These market failures may originate in moral hazard problems, which are more intense in some industries than in others, requiring that employers offer higher wages as an inducement for effective work. They might also originate in other factors such as market power on the part of unions.

Once there exist wage differentials that are arbitrary rather than based on skill differentials, it becomes possible that international integration—of trade or investment—may perversely make the domestic economy worse off, by shifting workers out of the good jobs. Suppose, for example, that foreign-based firms prefer for some reason to engage in high-wage activities at home, leaving only low-wage activities to be performed in the United States. Then their establishment of a large stake in the US economy will tend to reduce the number of high-wage jobs here, leaving the United States poorer as a whole.

We should note two points about this kind of argument. First, although the idea that foreign firms will keep the good jobs home strikes a nationalistic chord, it is in fact an empirical question. As we will see shortly, there is no evidence from US data that US affiliates of foreign firms do offer worse jobs than their domestically owned counterparts. Second, the argument is not at bottom a case against allowing FDI, but a case for having an explicit industrial policy to encourage high-wage jobs. Anyone strongly worried about the possibility that the United States will not have the right kind of employment should be a domestic industrial activist rather than an opponent of any foreign presence.

R&D and the Headquarters Effect

In discussing the potential benefits of FDI we emphasized the possibility that favorable external economies would result from spillovers of technology from the foreign firms. A concern that has been raised in the US context is that FDI might instead tend to reduce such favorable spillovers. The argument runs as follows: valuable externalities arise from the complex intellectual activities undertaken by firms, especially R&D. Firms, however, like to keep their sophisticated activities near the headquarters. When a firm with foreign headquarters acquires or displaces a US firm in the US market, it is therefore likely to shift the sophisticated activities abroad. The result is that US residents, who were previously able to derive indirect benefit from proximity to these activities, can no longer do so.

This is an economically impeccable argument. The only question is whether it is true. The argument has two parts: the assertion that certain identifiable activities yield valuable externalities, and the assumption that there is a strong "headquarters effect" that leads firms to concentrate these activities in their home country. Both of these are in principle empirical questions.

Unfortunately, the issue of externalities is not one that can be easily tackled in practice. External economies, by definition, do not leave a paper trail of market transactions by which they can be tracked and measured. Assessing the benefits from certain activities is therefore difficult, and this difficulty bedevils not only the assessment of FDI but virtually all discussions of competitiveness and industrial policy. We can add nothing here to that discussion except to note that we share the common prejudice that R&D is an activity fairly likely to yield positive externalities, although we cannot even guess at their magnitude.

If we accept that R&D is an item of special concern, we then have a more tractable problem in assessing the second part of the proposition: is there a strong headquarters effect? There has been extensive empirical study of the behavior of US and European multinationals in the past (see Cantwell 1989). The main result of this work is that, except in companies that have only recently become multinational, the headquarters effect is not strong. Experienced multinationals tend to place R&D activities in all of the major markets in which they participate; they show little tendency to concentrate R&D at home. We turn to the evidence on US affiliates of foreign firms later in this chapter.

Strategic Effects

The growth of Japanese investment in the United States has raised the possibility that FDI may be subject to the same kinds of strategic manipulation that recent theory has suggested is possible in international trade.

Recent trade theory has shown that in imperfectly competitive markets it is sometimes possible for government intervention to give domestic firms an advantage that enables them to extract high returns at the expense of foreign rivals. The essence of this theory of "strategic trade policy" runs as follows: suppose there is a world market in which, because of some kind of increasing returns, there is room for only a few firms to enter profitably. Then a government, either by offering domestic firms a subsidy or by closing the domestic market to foreign firms, can deter foreign firms from entering, thereby allowing domestic firms the opportunity to earn above-normal profits.[1]

There is a straightforward parallel in the case of FDI. Suppose there is an industry in which, because of the economies of scope associated with multinational operation, there is room for only a few multinational firms. Suppose also that Japanese firms are able to operate freely in the United States, but US firms do not receive national treatment and are unable to operate freely in Japan (as we have seen, Japan is indeed an outlier in terms of having very little inward FDI). Then, other things equal, a Japanese firm will have a strategic advantage over a US–based rival and may end up driving the US firm out of its home market as well as the protected Japanese market. In the same way that strategic trade policy can in principle act as a beggar-thy-neighbor policy that raises national income at foreign expense, so could an asymmetric FDI policy (see Graham 1989).

How seriously should this danger be taken? The strategic trade policy argument has been subject to extensive theoretical criticism, which has established that it is a possibility but by no means a general proposition that aggressive trade policies benefit the aggressor country. Efforts to quantify the potential gains from strategic trade policies indicate that these gains are small (Helpman and Krugman 1989). Since FDI in the United States is still a smaller factor than conventional integration through trade, we may suspect that the results carry over to an even greater extent here. It is hard to believe that the strategic disadvantages of US multinationals are a major drag on the US economy or will be one any time soon. Nonetheless, the strategic issue is one worth bearing in mind, and it gives some priority to US demands for parity of treatment in Japan in particular.

Characteristics of FDI in the United States

Foreign direct investment is no longer a marginal presence in the United States, and the question of how foreign firms will behave in the United States is therefore no longer a purely hypothetical one. We can ask how the many foreign firms already here behave, and compare their behavior with that of domestic firms. The largest question mark hangs over Japanese firms. Although Japanese FDI has been growing more rapidly than the aggregate, it is still relatively small and arguably not mature, especially in manufacturing. We will

---

1. See Brander and Spencer (1985) and the survey in Helpman and Krugman (1989).

Table 3.1 Employment and foreign trade of US multinational corporations and US affiliates of foreign firms, 1982

	US multinationals		Affiliates of foreign firms	
	All industries	Manu-facturing	All industries	Manu-facturing
Employment (thousands of workers)	18,704.6	10,532.3	2,448.1	1,241.6
Exports (millions of dollars)	153,225	105,202	60,236	12,883
Imports (millions of dollars)	110,961	42,853	84,290	12,386
Exports per worker (thousands of dollars)	8.19	9.99	24.61	10.38
Imports per worker (thousands of dollars)	5.93	4.06	34.43	9.98

Source: Survey of Current Business 66 (January and July 1986).

thus want to contrast Japanese and aggregate behavior, while bearing in mind that eventual Japanese behavior may look quite different.

In examining the characteristics of FDI, we want to focus in particular on those features that may shed some light on the possible negative effects of FDI. Does the behavior of US affiliates of foreign firms appear consistent with the kinds of scenario in which FDI is harmful, or does it look fairly innocent? We consider three features of FDI: the alleged high propensity of foreign-controlled firms to import due to a preference for foreign suppliers; their alleged tendency to keep the good jobs and the high-value production in their home countries; and the alleged headquarters effect that diminishes the extent of R&D and its favorable spillovers in the United States.

Foreign Trade

Table 3.1 compares the trade behavior in 1982 of two kinds of firms in the United States: parent companies of US–based multinationals and US affiliates of foreign firms. The table shows exports and imports per worker for all such firms and for manufacturing firms alone. A naive view would focus only on the data for all industries which show that, per employee, affiliates of foreign firms both imported and exported much more than their US counterparts. However, this emphasis is clearly misleading, because the firms covered by these data include firms that are essentially trading branches—marketing subsidiaries of Japanese auto companies, for example. It makes much more sense to focus on the manufacturing sector, where the behavior of foreign and US multinationals is much more similar. There is still, however, a significant behavioral difference: the affiliates of foreign firms did have an apparent tendency to import significantly more than US firms—almost two-and-a-half times as much.

This does not necessarily mean that if a foreign firm took over a US enterprise it would shift to foreign suppliers to the extent that imported inputs would increase by 150 percent. First, there remains a classification problem. In the data, an affiliate is classified as being in only one industry. For example, a foreign-owned firm that acts both as a marketing and distribution arm and as a manufacturing arm will be classified either under manufacturing or under wholesale trade. We have already noted that this may lead to some understatement of the size of the foreign role in manufacturing. It also definitely leads to some overstatement of import propensities within the manufacturing sector, because it means that even by focusing on manufacturing we have not eliminated the distorting effect of including foreign trading operations in the data.

In addition, some of the difference probably represents a selection bias in terms of activities within the manufacturing sector. In particular, to the extent that foreign firms that acquire or establish subsidiaries in the United States do so as part of a corporate strategy of forward integration, the particular activities into which foreign firms enter will tend to be import-intensive.

Finally, taking a look at foreign firms at a single point in time may yield a misleading picture. It is often argued that FDI in manufacturing typically begins with assembly operations that have low local content, but that over time there is increased local sourcing; this cycle is clearly apparent in the case of Japanese automobile manufacturing discussed below. Since foreign manufacturing in the United States has been growing rapidly, the data show a disproportionate number of relatively new foreign operations; their current high import propensity may substantially exaggerate the import propensity these same enterprises will have after they mature.

Despite these several reasons to discount the high apparent tendency of foreign-owned firms in the United States to import, we have not been able to recalculate the reported numbers to adjust for these effects. The raw facts do support the stereotype that foreign firms import more, and our guess is that even if all plausible corrections were made, this qualitative fact would remain.

What are the costs to the United States of this higher import propensity? To the extent that the additional imports really represent a net increase—in other words, ignoring the extent to which production by foreign firms may substitute for imports or add to exports—the effect is to require a lower value of the US dollar to achieve any given trade balance. It is possible to estimate an upper bound on this effect by assuming that all of the difference between imports of foreign and domestic manufacturers represents a negative effect on the US trade

Table 3.2 Value added and compensation per employee among US affiliates of foreign firms, 1986 (thousands of dollars)

Industry	Value added		Compensation[a]	
	US affiliates	All US firms	US affiliates	All US firms
All industries[b]	49.2	47.5	29.2	25.7
Mining	93.0	67.9	45.4	39.6
Petroleum	151.0	161.9	41.7	44.7
Manufacturing	46.6	44.8	32.9	32.6
Food and kindred products	41.5	46.6	24.4	27.9
Chemicals and allied products	60.7	69.5	36.2	40.0
Primary and fabricated metals	44.0	43.4	36.3	33.1
Machinery	36.7	40.0	33.1	33.3
Other manufacturing	44.3	44.2	31.7	32.1
Wholesale trade	67.3	53.2	32.4	30.2
Retail trade	21.0	27.1	13.6	16.3
Finance, insurance, and real estate[c]	52.3	141.3	50.6	31.9
Banking	n.a.	49.7	n.a.	27.8
All other industries[b]	50.1	54.0	22.4	24.4

a. Includes wages, salaries, benefits. b. Excluding government. c. Excluding banking.

Sources: Calculated from tables in Bureau of Economic Analysis, "Foreign Direct Investment in the United States: Gross Product of Nonbank U.S. Affiliates of Foreign Companies, 1977–86" (mimeographed, 23 August 1988); Foreign Direct Investment in the United States: Operations of U.S. Affiliates of Foreign Companies: Preliminary 1986 Estimates" (June 1988); and "National Income and Product Accounts," *Survey of Current Business* 68 (July 1988).

balance. Then we can use the comparison in table 3.1 to derive the size of the required decline in the dollar.

According to table 3.1, in 1982 the typical foreign manufacturing multinational imported approximately $10,000 worth of materials per worker versus only $4,000 per worker for domestically owned firms. By 1990 there will be approximately 2 million US residents working for foreign-owned manufacturers. This comparison suggests that if these firms had remained domestically owned, imports in 1990 at any given exchange rate would have been approximately $12 billion lower in 1982 prices (assuming per-worker imports of both types of firm have not changed since 1982). If one allows for the rise in traded-goods prices since 1982, the amount is about $15 billion.

Standard estimates of the effect of the exchange rate on trade suggest that a 1 percent fall in the dollar will reduce the US trade deficit, other things equal, by at least $5 billion (Cline 1989). Thus, *on the most pessimistic estimate* the total effect of foreign ownership of US manufacturing has been to reduce the equilibrium value of the dollar by 3 percent. Bearing in mind that there was some foreign ownership in US manufacturing even in the late 1970s, and given the limits to using apparent differences in import propensities as a measure of trade impact, it is unlikely that the growth of foreign ownership of US manufacturing since 1980 has reduced the equilibrium value of the dollar by more than about 1 percent.

Thus, although it is undeniable that foreign-owned firms in the United States have a higher propensity to import than their US—owned counterparts, this is not a good argument to prove substantial economic harm from FDI, politically sensitive though the issue may be. This difference in import behavior is in fact the *only* significant behavioral difference between foreign and US firms that we will find.

Wages and Value Added

Table 3.2 compares compensation per employee and value added per employee across industries for affiliates of foreign firms against US firms as a whole. The striking and at first surprising result is that both compensation and value added per worker are actually higher for affiliates of foreign firms than for the average US firm. However, a look further down the table reveals that the difference is essentially due to differences in composition. Specifically, the heavy concentration of FDI in high-wage, capital-intensive sectors such as petroleum and banking raises the average. For manufacturing as a whole, and for individual sectors within manufacturing, there is no systematic difference between the foreign and the domestic firms in compensation and value added per employee. These data thus do not provide any support for the view that foreign firms typically keep the good jobs or the high-value-added activities at home.

Research and Development

Table 3.3 compares R&D by all US firms and affiliates of foreign firms for 1983, the last year for which comparable data were available. As the table indicates, R&D per worker was actually much higher for affiliates of foreign firms than for the US economy as a whole. However, this again largely reflects the difference in composition between foreign-owned enterprise and the national economy. The great bulk of measured private R&D in the United States occurs in the manufacturing sector, which accounted for more than half the employment by foreign firms but only 20 percent of total US employment. The comparison of R&D per worker in manufacturing alone shows roughly comparable numbers. The slightly larger number for the foreign firms may reflect a concentration in high-technology industries.

Table 3.3   Research and development by US affiliates of foreign firms, 1983

	R&D (millions of dollars)	Employment (thousands of workers)	R&D per worker (thousands of dollars)
All industries			
Affiliates	4,164	2,546	1.64
US firms	42,600	90,200	0.47
Manufacturing			
Affiliates	3,553	1,321	2.69
US firms	41,583	18,434	2.26

Sources: affiliates: Bureau of Economic Analysis, "Foreign Direct Investment in the United States: Operations of U.S. Affiliates of Foreign Companies," 1983 estimates; US firms—National Science Foundation, *Science Indicators: 1983* (Washington: National Science Foundation).

Like the data on compensation and value added, the data on R&D do not provide any indication that foreign firms behave differently from US firms in a way that could be viewed as detrimental to the US economy. In particular, there is no sign of a headquarters effect that leads foreign firms to perform R&D at home rather than in the United States.

Are Japanese Firms Different?

Our survey of evidence on how foreign firms behave in the United States finds, broadly speaking, that they look a lot like US firms: they are comparable in terms of value added, compensation, and R&D per worker. Except for the ambiguous fact of a greater propensity to import, there is nothing in the evidence to justify concerns about the economic impact of an increased foreign role.

In the public mind, however, there is an important distinction among firms of different nationalities. Many US citizens and policymakers may be willing to accept the idea that British, Dutch, and Canadian firms act much like American firms, and indeed in many cases they may for all practical purposes *be* American firms. Many concerns about inward FDI, however, are focused on Japanese firms. As we have seen, these firms still account for a small fraction of the foreign presence in the United States, and their share has not been rising very rapidly (except in 1988). Still, there is a question whether the growing Japanese presence is qualitatively different.

There are several reasons why one might suspect that Japanese firms would behave differently from other firms with affiliates in the United States. One is the difference in the nature of the home base: as we saw in table 1.8, Japanese firms appear to be much more sheltered than firms in other industrial nations from foreign competition in their home market (although this may change as Japan liberalizes its markets). Institutionally, Japanese firms are structured very differently from firms elsewhere, with their participation in *keiretsu* (business groups), their very long-term relations with employees, and in other ways. There is also a widespread belief that Japanese firms can be induced through the "invisible handshake" to act in ways that the Japanese government believes serve the national interest, even when this does not maximize their profits.

The question is whether these fears about differences in Japanese firms' behavior are grounded. Since Japanese FDI represents a much smaller and somewhat more recent sample than overall FDI, the lessons of Japanese experience are not as solid as those for foreign firms in general. Nonetheless, it is useful to compare the evidence on the behavior of Japanese affiliates with that of foreign-controlled firms on average.

Table 3.4 presents some comparisons. In a number of ways the comparison resembles that between affiliates of foreign firms and US firms. At the aggregate level, Japanese firms in the United States have substantially higher than average gross product per worker, exports, and imports, and substantially lower R&D per worker. However, most of these differences may be attributed to differences in composition, as Japanese FDI is relatively concentrated in marketing arms of overseas firms and in the capital-intensive financial sector, and has a relatively small presence in manufacturing. In the manufacturing sector, compensation, value added, and R&D levels are essentially the same as for other affiliates of foreign firms. (The R&D figure is that for total private R&D per manufacturing worker, because the BEA does not provide the numbers for manufacturing broken out by country. However, since the great bulk of private R&D takes place in the manufacturing sector, this does not do much harm.)

The only major difference between Japanese and other foreign manufacturing firms is a higher Japanese import propensity: about 2.5 to 1, just like the comparison of affiliates and US multinationals. Why should this be the case? There may be a national bias involved: Japanese firms may be pressured to continue relying on domestic suppliers, or may simply not trust US suppliers, to a greater extent than other foreign investors. However, we speculate that the main reason is related to the mismeasurement of marketing firms as manufacturers and the selection bias that leads foreign firms to enter the US disproportionately in activities that make use of imported inputs; these factors may be at work in Japanese FDI, which is newer and less mature, to a greater degree than among foreign investors as a whole. Numerous studies of the behavior of multinational firms indicate that as these firms become more experienced in the conduct of international operations they tend to increase the local content of the output of their overseas subsidiaries (see, e.g., Vernon 1966). Because Japanese firms are typically quite inexperienced in the role of foreign direct investors, it is

Table 3.4   Characteristics of US affiliates of Japanese firms, 1986[a]

	All foreign affiliates		Japanese affiliates	
	Totals (millions of dollars)	Per worker (thousands of dollars)	Totals (millions of dollars)	Per worker (thousands of dollars)
All industries				
Value added[b]	145,977	49.24	14,139	65.34
Compensation	86,631	29.22	6,755	31.22
Exports	50,713	17.11	22,693	104.87
Imports	124,476	41.99	63,724	294.48
R&D	5,539	1.87	325	1.50
Manufacturing				
Value added[b]	65,282	46.64	3,199	47.39
Compensation	46,029	32.89	2,362	34.99
Exports	12,573	8.98	906	13.42
Imports	20,791	14.85	2,936	43.48
R&D[c]	n.a.	3.96	n.a.	4.81
Memorandum: employment (thousands of workers)				
All industries	2,964.5		216.4	
Manufacturing	1,399.6		67.5	

n.a. = not available.

a. Preliminary.

b. Per-worker figures are in terms of gross product per worker.

c. Total private R&D per worker.

Sources: Bureau of Economic Analysis, "Foreign Direct Investment in the United States: Operations of U.S. Affiliates of Foreign Companies," various tables; "Foreign Direct Investment in the United States: Gross Product of Nonbank Affiliates of Foreign Companies," various tables.

reasonable to expect them to increase the domestic content of their US subsidiaries' output as they gain experience.

The example of Japanese investment in the US automobile industry usefully illustrates this point. Japanese investment in this industry began with assembly plants, which initially relied heavily on traditional suppliers: the autos assembled by Honda and Nissan in the United States initially had domestic contents of only 30 and 47 percent, respectively, as compared with more than 90 percent in autos produced by US manufacturers. Over time, however, relationships have been established with US suppliers and Japanese suppliers have moved to the United States, allowing a rising domestic content. In 1987 Honda and Nissan reported local content of 60 and 63 percent, respectively, and both expect to have 75 percent local content or more by the early 1990s (US General Accounting Office 1988).

The case of color televisions, discussed in Chapter 2, is another useful example. US firms responded to the Japanese entry into this market with heavy overseas sourcing, even as Japanese firms increased their US production; in the face of the technological superiority of the Japanese, it was the US firms that placed the most weight on low labor costs. The result was that by the mid-1980s the remaining US firms were less American in their production than their Japanese competitors.

In any case, as we have argued, a high import propensity is not a clear economic cost. The surprising result is that the idea that Japanese firms keep sophisticated, high-value activities at home is simply not borne out by the data.

The "Fire Sale" Issue

Although our survey of the evidence does not in general support fears that foreign firms will behave differently from US firms in ways that are detrimental to the US economy, there is still one more argument against inward FDI that must be considered. This is the argument, identified with Mundell (1987) and Rohatyn (1988), among others, that foreign firms are currently acquiring a large stake in the US economy at an excessively low price because of the low value of the dollar. The argument that the United States is holding a "fire sale" of its assets has struck a chord with many, raising worries that the United States is mortgaging its future by accepting FDI now.

For the fire sale argument to be valid, two things must be true. First, the dollar must now be undervalued, in the sense that the market is making a mistake and that there will be large capital gains for those who buy US assets now. Second, the undervaluation of the dollar, if it has occurred, must lead US residents to make some kind of exchange at unfavorable terms of trade.

The proposition that the dollar is grossly undervalued is stated by Rohatyn and others without much attempt at justification. To assert this proposition requires that one dismiss several counterarguments. The first is that the market does not agree with the proposition; if it did, the dollar would not be where it is. The second is that the claim of massive dollar undervaluation is not supported by simple indices of US competitive position, which generally show the US relative cost and price position to be about where it was in 1980. The third is that econometric studies of international trade adjustment have almost universally concluded that the current level of the dollar is still too high to induce a closing of international current account imbalances—a result supported by the stalling of trade balance improvement in mid-1989.

The one currency with respect to which there is some indication that the dollar is undervalued is the yen: in this case purchasing power parities for traded goods indicate that a return to 1980 levels would yield a yen at about 180 to the dollar, or about a one-third rise in the dollar from present levels. Against this calculation one may note that the Japanese current account remains in massive surplus, and that a substantial secular upward trend in the equilibrium yen is both apparent in econometric work and reasonable given Japanese technological progress. In brief, only vis-à-vis the yen can one make a case for a greatly undervalued dollar, and even there much of the evidence points the other way.

Suppose, however, that one accepts for the sake of argument the view that the dollar is greatly undervalued against the yen. This is still not enough to establish that a fire sale of US assets is taking place. One must examine both sides of the transaction: when foreigners invest in the United States, what are US residents getting in return? It is the terms of trade on this exchange, not the exchange rate, that measures the price that the United States is getting for its assets.

Foreign nations can pay for US assets either by shipping us goods and services or by selling us assets in return. In fact they have done both: while the United States has run large current account deficits, and thus has been a heavy net importer of capital, US outward investment has continued.

Have the terms on which US assets have been exchanged for foreign goods and services been so unusually poor as to constitute a fire sale? The prices of imports into the United States relative to the prices of domestic goods have not been historically high in recent years; indeed, relative import prices have stayed surprisingly low despite a declining dollar (Hooper and Mann 1987). Nor have US assets been unusually cheap relative to the domestic price level, with the stock market still high despite the October 1987 crash. Thus, there is no argument to be made that the exchange of assets for goods represents a bad deal for the United States. In other words, that part of the gross increase in foreign assets in the United States that was paid for by the US current account deficit is exempt from the fire sale argument.

The fire sale argument only makes sense, then, to the extent that foreigners were able to persuade US residents to give up undervalued US assets in return for foreign assets. To put it another way, the fire sale argument may be reduced to the argument that the United States has a predictable capital loss on its own overseas investment. In 1987 foreign assets in the United States increased by $221 billion; only $76 billion of this increase was matched by US acquisitions of assets abroad. The fire sale argument applies, if at all, to the possibility of a capital loss on that $76 billion.

Further, not all of US capital outflow can be reasonably proposed, even for the sake of argument, to be subject to a predictable capital loss. Indeed, only for Japan is there a strong—and still highly disputable—case to be made for serious dollar undervaluation. Thus the potential fire sale loss should be restricted to capital losses on US investment in Japan. In 1987 US private investors placed $24 billion in Japan. If the dollar is "really" worth 180 yen, there is a predictable capital loss of about 25 percent on a purchase of yen-denominated assets. This implies an estimate of the fire sale component to foreign investment in the United States of about $6 billion. Notice that this applies to foreign investment generally, and not specifically to direct investment; it makes no real difference to the cost whether the foreigners are buying firms or Treasury bills.

On the most pessimistic reasonable assumptions, then, which we do not share, the cost to the United States of the fire sale due to a weak dollar amounted to $6 billion in 1987. This is not a trivial sum, although it is a hypothetical and speculative one. It certainly falls far short of justifying the apocalyptic rhetoric of Rohatyn, in particular.

Conclusions

A careful assessment of the evidence on FDI in the United States does not justify great concern about its effects. Foreign firms do not shift high-value or high-compensation activities to their home countries, nor do they perform less R&D in the United States than their US counterparts. Their only discernible difference is a higher propensity to import, which may represent a difference in behavior but may instead represent a selection bias in the activities in which foreign firms engage. There is little in this evidence to suggest that affiliates of foreign firms make less of a contribution to the US economy than do US–owned firms in the same industry.

Japanese firms show surprisingly little difference in their behavior from other foreign firms. Their value added and compensation per worker are similar to those of other foreign firms, as is their R&D effort in the United States. The only difference is a still-higher apparent propensity to import, which may be the result of a selection bias.

The frequent argument that foreign firms are buying into the US economy too cheaply does not stand up under careful analysis. If it makes any sense at all, it represents a fairly limited cost rather than a wholesale sellout of US assets at fire sale prices.

4

Political Effects

Up to this point we have focused on the purely economic consequences of foreign direct investment in the United States. In practice, however, many of the concerns regarding growing inward FDI are political concerns: the worry that a substantial presence of foreign-owned firms will distort the domestic political process.

The question of the political role of foreign-owned firms operating in the United States is sometimes seen as part of a broader issue, that of foreign influence on US policy generally; that is, it is seen in the context of foreign lobbying over US trade policy, government-to-government negotiations, and so on. We have considerable sympathy with this view and will come back to some of the linkages in Chapter 7. For now, however, we want to focus on the issues raised specifically by foreign ownership of US firms.

Even with this limitation, this is a large subject, and one that is less well structured than the economics of FDI proper. We will not endeavor to provide anything like a complete survey of the political aspects of international investment; such a survey would be outside both our competence and the reasonable bounds of this study. Instead, we offer an economist's-eye view of the problem, concentrating on three key points that seem to us crucial.

The first point is, strictly speaking, an economic rather than a political observation: when there is substantial foreign ownership of domestic factors of production, the evaluation of economic policies from a national point of view may be quite different from what it would be otherwise. Policies such as provision of subsidies or protection may have the effect of redistributing income to these foreign-owned factors, and thus will be more costly to the nation, perhaps by a large margin, than they would be in the absence of foreign ownership.

The second point is that the foreign owners of domestic factors, like owners of any factors, will try to influence the domestic political process to follow policies that they like. If successful, they will redistribute income away from domestic residents toward foreign, whereas successful manipulation of the political process domestically only redistributes income among domestic residents. This is the sense in which foreign influence on the political process may be a source of greater concern than influence by domestic special-interest groups.

Is this greater concern really justified? The third point is that foreign influence only adds another imperfection to a political system that is already highly inefficient. Indeed, even without the involvement of foreign multinationals, the US political system quite often implements policies that transfer rents to foreigners (an example is the extensive reliance on export restraints administered by foreign governments to protect US domestic industries) or otherwise impose large net losses on domestic residents. Thus, fears about foreign influence may be contrasting a worst-case scenario with an idealized depiction of actual US policymaking.

Strategic Effects of Foreign Ownership

The standard cost-benefit analysis used in public finance and international trade policy alike draws a sharp distinction between the redistributive effects of policies and their efficiency effects. While everyone knows that the distributive effects of a policy are often politically decisive, the economic analysis of policies usually focuses on the efficiency gains and losses.

Consider, to take a concrete example, the case of a tariff. Suppose that a country imposes a tariff on a good that it can import from the rest of the world at a fixed price. Then the tariff affects the real incomes of three domestic groups: consumers, producers, and the government. Consumers lose from the higher import price, producers gain from the higher domestic price, and the government collects some tariff revenue. It is a standard exercise to show that because the tariff distorts production and consumption decisions, the consumer loss exceeds the gains to producers and the government, so that there is a net loss to the economy as a whole. However, this net loss is ordinarily much smaller than the cost to consumers, most of which is offset by gains to the government or to producers.

The usual working assumption in cost-benefit analysis is that redistributions may be netted out. Everyone is a producer of something and a consumer of something else, and in any case income distribution is accomplished to at least some degree by the existing program of taxation and social insurance policies. So, as a first approximation, it is usual to argue that the economist's job is to focus on the costs and benefits that are not pure redistributions from one group to another. In the case of a tariff, this means that the cost of the tariff is measured by the net loss that results from production and consumption distortions. One then compares this net loss with whatever objective the tariff is supposed to serve and asks whether the benefits in fact exceed the costs.

Obviously this is not even a caricature of the actual political process by which US trade policy is made. Leaving that issue for later discussion, however, we may ask how the picture changes if there is foreign ownership of some part of domestic industry. The answer is that, from a national point of view, redistributions cannot be netted out, since those benefiting from (or hurt by) them may be foreign rather than domestic residents.

This point may be made most strongly if we imagine that the industry is entirely foreign owned. Then, from the domestic point of view, the entire producer gain represents a net cost; the national cost of the tariff becomes the consumer cost less any government revenue. If foreigners own only a share of the industry, only part of the producer gain will represent a national loss, but the principle is the same.

For moderate tariff rates the efficiency effects of a tariff are typically small relative to its redistributive effects. This means that in any industry where foreign firms control a substantial part of production, the redistributive effects of policy toward or away from these firms will typically be a more important issue for national welfare than the efficiency gains or losses with which economists are usually preoccupied.

From a world point of view matters look quite different: gains to foreign-owned firms still represent a redistribution rather than a loss. To the extent that a country is a home country as well as a host country for multinational firms, it may prefer rules of the game that prevent countries from worrying too much about international redistributive effects, even if these rules constrain its own actions. This is a point that we will return to; meanwhile, let us note three implications of the redistributive effects of policies on foreign-owned factors.

First, the cost (or possibly the benefit) of a policy may be much larger because of foreign ownership of factors of production than it would be otherwise. A tariff or a subsidy to an industry will impose higher national costs if the benefits go largely to foreigners rather than to domestic firms and workers. Conversely, some policies, such as deregulation of a largely foreign-owned industry or import liberalization where the affected domestic producers are foreign owned, may in effect legally expropriate foreign holdings, producing national gains over and above any efficiency consequences.

Second, foreign capital inflows may exacerbate the consequences of distortional policies. For example, a tariff that protects capital-intensive sectors will create high returns for investors in these sectors. If foreign capital moves in as a consequence, the foreign investors may well receive earnings that exceed the true contribution their capital has made to national product, leaving the country worse off (see Brecher and Diaz-Alejandro 1977 for a demonstration of this in a standard trade model).

Third, to the extent that foreign owners of factors of production can influence the domestic political process in their favor, the net national costs will tend to be larger than if domestic firms do the same. The reason is not that foreigners behave any differently, but simply that they and not domestic residents appropriate the gains. If a US firm is able to engineer tariff protection for itself, much of the cost to consumers represents an internal redistribution within the United States; if a foreign firm does the same, the redistribution represents a decline in US national income.

The important point, then, is that the economic impact of political activity by foreign-owned firms will be somewhat different from that of similar activity by domestically owned firms. This will be true even if the firms otherwise behave similarly, which is what we would expect.

Political Influence of Foreign-Owned Firms

In much of the world, multinational firms are viewed as possessing political power disproportionate to that of domestic interest groups. This view is fed by the size of large multinationals relative to indigenous firms in small countries, and by the view that firms from advanced countries are in some degree agents of their powerful home governments (or vice versa).

It is questionable whether this view of multinationals as uniquely powerful and dangerous makes much sense even in small countries. For the United States it is clearly unreasonable to think of foreign-owned firms as qualitatively different political actors from those already on the scene. The United States already has large firms, trade associations, unions, and the like attempting to influence policy. Some foreign firms in the United States compare in scale to their domestic counterparts; only a few are massively larger. Likewise, the US government is not going to become a minor player compared with other advanced-country governments anytime in the near future.

The point, then, is not that foreign-owned firms will play a different political game from domestic interest groups, but that the game will have different outcomes. That is, the concern will be that foreign firms will at least sometimes succeed in influencing the political process in ways that redistribute income away from the United States.

How might the political process be influenced? Foreign firms do not, of course, vote. However, they may influence decision making either directly, through the use of resources to influence voting and legislation, or indirectly, by using their bargaining power to extract special treatment.

There is no generally accepted formal model of the ways in which financial resources may be used to influence political outcomes, even though the existence of the phenomenon is hardly controversial. Aside from straightforward corruption on the part of appointed or elected officials, such expenditures can affect political outcomes primarily because of the public-goods aspects of the political process. Voters do not have much individual incentive to act politically on or even to become informed about issues that have only a small per capita impact, even if in the aggregate these issues matter a great deal. Therefore, an interested party that can mobilize a small group of activists, provide campaign funds to officials seeking reelection, or offer highly visible benefits to some voters may be able to get a policy enacted that is not in the interest of the majority of voters. It is a commonplace that small, well-organized groups often get public policies enacted that benefit them at substantial but thinly spread cost to the general public; the examples range from sugar producers to thrift institutions.

This commonplace applies to interest groups in general, not foreign investors in particular. Foreign firms will not play this game any better than domestic groups—indeed they will normally be at some disadvantage, both because of lack of familiarity with the rules and because they encounter some hostility precisely because they are foreign. When they do play the game successfully, however, they redistribute income out of the country instead of simply within it.

A more easily modeled example of political influence is the way in which a firm may induce governments to compete for a desirable investment. Suppose that a foreign firm has decided to locate a facility in the United States that, it is believed, will yield valuable external benefits to the region in which it is located. Suppose also that the foreign firm regards a number of US locations as roughly equally suitable. Then the candidate states and localities may well compete to attract the foreign firm, with tax breaks, provision of infrastructure, and perhaps outright subsidy. The effect of this competition will be to dissipate any national gains from the spillovers, transferring them to the foreign firm instead.

Expensive competition among states and localities to attract foreign firms has become a real issue in recent years. For example, the Mazda assembly plant in Flat Rock, Michigan, was lured by a 14-year waiver of property taxes, and the Toyota plant in Kentucky by state provision of free land, $47 million in new roads, and $65 million in employee training programs (Jackson 1987). Some have argued that such interstate competition is more intense for foreign investments than for similar investments by domestic firms, because the foreign investments are more visible and attract more media attention, and hence generate more political points for politicians who succeed in luring them. Whether or not foreign firms actually do better than domestic firms in such bidding wars, those wars are more costly to the United States as a whole than similar bidding for a domestic firm's presence.

Thus, political influence by foreign firms can in principle be a source of economic costs to the United States. The questions that remain are how important those costs are and how much difference foreign influence really makes to the costs imposed by other self-punishing policies.

How Much Does It Matter?

We have identified some reasons why domestic policies that redistribute income to foreign-owned firms will have a larger cost from a US point of view than similar policies that benefit only domestic firms, and we have briefly discussed the channels of political influence that may lead to policies that redistribute income out of the country. The key question, however, is how much those losses matter. Should we expect the political system to yield outcomes that are significantly worse, from the point of view of domestic residents, than before foreign firms became an important part of the economy?

It is crucial not to start from an idealized description of policy in the absence of foreign firms. Ideally, economic policy is carried out in such a way as to minimize deadweight costs—costs, such as inefficiencies or transfers to foreigners, that hurt one group without benefiting another group within the country. If policy were efficient in this sense, then adding foreign owners of factors of production to the process fundamentally alters it, because only then would the struggle over distribution have as a possible outcome a reduction in national income.

In practice, however, US economic policies already often impose large, unnecessary deadweight costs, whether because of distortion of incentives or because the policy ends up redistributing income out of the country even when foreign firms have no say in the matter. Given that the existing process produces such self-punishing results, one should not overstress the extra concern that arises from the presence of foreign-owned firms.

Two familiar examples may make the point. The first is the case of US trade policy toward automobiles. Within the next few years US affiliates of Japanese firms are expected to constitute a substantial fraction of the domestic auto industry. These affiliates will presumably attempt to affect the domestic political process in their favor. However, it is difficult to imagine that they would induce a more self-punishing policy than the actual US policy over the past decade. US protection of the automobile industry was in principle aimed at protecting employment; the textbook answer would have been to subsidize that employment directly. Instead, the United States adopted a voluntary trade restraint that distorted consumer choice, reduced competition in the domestic industry because the policy imposed a fixed quantitative restriction, and actually transferred the quota rents to the Japanese. Thus, some of the consumer cost of the auto import quota leaked away either into inefficiency or as benefits to foreigners rather than being transferred to domestic producers. Had some of the US industry been foreign-owned at that point the costs would have been even larger, but the policy might not have been the same.

The second example is that of regulation in banking and finance, a sector where Japanese banks have been playing a large role. It is certainly possible that at some future date Japanese financial institutions in the United States will lobby successfully for some change in regulation that benefits them at the expense of US residents in general. However, it is hard to imagine that any such change could be as costly to US residents as the misregulation of the wholly domestic thrift industry, where the combination of deregulation and deposit insurance has led to massive misallocation of resources, only some of which has shown up as gains to thrift owners.

In general, US microeconomic policy, like that of virtually all countries, is full of examples of policies that redistribute income very inefficiently, imposing large net costs either through distortion of economic decisions or through losses to foreigners. We need only note that of the four major industries that have received import protection from the United States during the 1980s (automobiles, steel, textiles and apparel, and sugar), *all* have been protected through arrangements that transfer what might have been tariff revenue to foreigners.

The reasons for this apparent preference for inefficient policies probably lie in the same factors that allow interest groups to affect the political process in the first place: the free-rider problem of getting voters mobilized and the cost of information. An interest group may prefer an inefficient policy such as a voluntary export restraint (VER) to an efficient one such as a direct subsidy, even though the VER imposes higher costs on the general public, because those costs are less visible.

The question of how to reform the political process so as to minimize this kind of costly distortion—and the question of how much inefficiency is an inevitable part of any political process—lie far beyond the scope of this study. Our point is simply that a realistic view of how public policies are set should discourage our attributing a special character to political activity by foreign firms. This is not to deny that there is a real issue at stake: a foreign firm that is able to influence national policy in its own interest is somewhat more likely to have a negative effect on national welfare, other things equal, than a domestic firm exerting similar influence. However, in practice national welfare is reduced by most successful attempts to influence policies by any special interest, foreign or domestic. In the real, imperfect policy environment, in which bad decisions are made and lived with all the time, adding some foreign influence represents only a minor change.

International Rules of the Game

We pointed out earlier in this chapter that the redistributive effects of policies when there are foreign-owned factors of production look quite different from a world point of view than from the point of view of a single country. A policy that redistributes income toward foreign-owned factors is a cost from the national but not from the global point of view, and correspondingly, a policy that reduces foreign firms' income benefits the home country but not the world.

This immediately tells us that international investment must take place under some explicit or implicit rules of the game that limit the extent to which countries can take a parochial view that regards income earned by foreigners as a pure loss. In general, world income will be maximized when factors of production are treated the same whatever their ownership, and in particular, when multinational firms are treated in the same way as domestic firms.

This view has in fact been the standard US position, dating from a time when the United States was much more likely to be on the receiving than the giving end of policies against foreign firms. The traditional US position is one that advocates right of establishment together with national treatment; that is, a firm from one country should have the unimpeded ability to establish subsidiaries in other countries, and once established, these subsidiaries should receive the same treatment as domestic firms. Together, these rights would in effect establish neutrality of policy with respect to the nationality of a firm's owners.

This position was a natural one for the United States to take when it played a one-sided role as a home rather than a host for multinationals; the advantage to the United States of a code of behavior that allowed its own firms free operation abroad was obvious. However, there are still advantages to such a code even in the more symmetric situation of today. First, the United States is still a major home for multinationals, and it would lose as much as it gained if there were widespread adoption of nationalistic policies aimed against foreign firms. Second, although it may be advantageous to pursue economic policies that reduce the earnings of foreign firms *ex post*, once those firms are already established, a country would like to assure investors *ex ante* that this will not happen, so as to attract beneficial capital inflows. An international code that ensures national treatment is one way to make such an assurance credible.

We discuss the possible outline of such an international code in Chapter 7. Here we simply note that the political economy of FDI cannot be addressed purely as a matter of unilateral US policy.

5

National Security Concerns

Of the issues posed by the operations of foreign-based multinationals in the United States, those relating to national security are among the most difficult. Whereas many of the purely economic implications of foreign direct investment are no more serious than the routine problems that occur in virtually all areas of economic policy, in the national security arena special problems arise from conflicts between the objectives of different nations.

There are two quite different situations in which the national security implications of FDI can become an issue. One is that of potential or actual military conflict between the host country and the home country of a multinational enterprise. FDI has been a problem in such circumstances in the past but, we will argue, seems unlikely to be a major problem in the foreseeable future. The other situation is where the foreign affiliate's home country is a friendly nation but foreign ownership is deemed nonetheless to impair the host nation's defense capability.

We examine each of these situations in this chapter. We conclude the chapter by outlining a few other issues regarding FDI and national security that we see as relevant to US policy concerns but that are not yet wholly resolved. Our policy recommendations relating to national security and FDI are to be found in Chapter 7.

FDI and National Security in Time of War or National Emergency

The threat of FDI to a host country's national security becomes most acute when the host finds itself at war or in a state of national emergency, which we define as circumstances that could lead imminently to war. We concentrate in this chapter on the case in which a parent firm based in the country with which the host nation is at war or about to go to war controls a subsidiary in the host nation. We defer discussion of the security implications of the imminent takeover of domestically controlled firms by foreign firms until Chapter 6, where we discuss the recently enacted Exon-Florio amendment.

Table 5.1 Foreign direct investment by security relationship to the United States of country of ultimate beneficial owner, 1987

Security status	Direct investment position (billions of dollars)	Percentage of total FDI
NATO members	178.5	68.2
Non-NATO Western Europe and other US allies[a]	61.0	23.3
Total allies	239.5	91.5
Eastern bloc	0.1	0.04
All others	22.3	8.5
Total for all nations	261.9	100.04[b]

a. Includes Japan, Australia, and New Zealand.

b. Percentages do not sum to 100.0 because of rounding.

Source: "Foreign Direct Investment in the United States: Detail for Position and Balance of Payments," *Survey of Current Business* 68 (August 1988), 69.

When analyzing the national security implications of FDI it is helpful to have a sense of the present political geography of FDI in the United States. Table 5.1 shows the aggregate stocks of FDI held in the United States by nations in the following categories: members of the North Atlantic Treaty Organization (NATO); non–NATO Western European nations and members of other multilateral military alliances with the United States; Eastern bloc nations; and all others. The table shows that the vast bulk of FDI in the United States is held by nations in the first two categories, which consist of those nations that are friendly to the United States and that few would view as likely military opponents in the foreseeable future. The only nations that might be considered potential US adversaries fall into the third and fourth categories; these account for only a small portion of total FDI in the United States.

Even though very little FDI in the United States comes from nations that could be labeled enemies or potential enemies, it is nevertheless worthwhile to examine the issue of actual or possible military conflict between the home and host nations of a multinational firm. The national security issues pertaining to FDI are at their starkest under circumstances of actual conflict and are to a great extent the same issues that are raised under less extreme circumstances, for example when tensions exist between the home and the host country that are unlikely to lead to war but nonetheless cause relations between the two to sour.

Relations between the United States and France during the late 1960s provide an example. At that time there was considerable tension between the two countries, even though relations never remotely approached a state of open conflict. One reason for the tension was the United States' effort to use French subsidiaries of US–based multinational enterprises to further US policy objectives, which at the time were often in conflict with French objectives. In particular, the United States instructed these subsidiaries to withhold technology from the French military as a means to pressure France to be more supportive of US policy in Vietnam. Consequently, during that period, the French seriously questioned whether it was appropriate for local subsidiaries of US–based firms to be closely involved with the French national defense effort, and indeed the French government took steps to create independent sources of certain products and technologies that were then heavily dominated by US producers. (See Moran 1989 for details of this period.)

Today no such level of tension exists between the United States and any of the countries that are major homes to FDI in the United States; nonetheless, some tension does exist with certain of these home countries, and the possibility is always there that it will increase. We therefore examine three questions pertaining to FDI in times of military conflict or national emergency that could lead to military conflict and ask what, if any, lessons can be drawn.

The first question is whether the overseas subsidiaries of multinational enterprises based in an unfriendly nation will tend to act as a "fifth column" on behalf of the home country. That is, will the subsidiary act as an agent of the home country to reduce the war preparedness of the host country?

Second, will the breaking of managerial links between the parent firm and the subsidiary in time of actual war damage the ability of the subsidiary to contribute to the war effort of the host country? This question is intimately linked to the fifth-column issue, and so to some extent we discuss the two questions concurrently.

Third, is the United States well or at least adequately protected against the eventuality that foreign-controlled subsidiaries might act as fifth columns or otherwise jeopardize the national security in time of war or imminent war?

Foreign Affiliates as Fifth Columns

Possible fifth-column activities of multinational firms include not only overt espionage and other unfriendly acts, but also certain less obviously hostile acts. For example, the subsidiary might leak sensitive but nonclassified information to the parent in circumstances short of war, before links between subsidiary and parent are broken. Such leakage, although harmful to the host country, would fall short of outright espionage. The subsidiary could also act as a "passive" fifth column simply by not producing war matériel at rates or of the quality of which it is capable.

It is difficult to generalize about the prevalence of fifth-column behavior on the part of foreign-owned subsidiaries. A few historical examples serve to illustrate that the outcome can go either way: there have been cases in which subsidiaries have indeed behaved as agents of their home governments in times of conflict, and there have been cases that offer little evidence of such behavior. One point that does emerge, however, is that fifth-column-like behavior by local subsidiaries is more likely in circumstances that fall short of actual war than during war itself.

During World War II, for example, the Ford Motor Company owned subsidiaries in both Germany and Great Britain. Examination of the conduct of the subsidiaries' operations during the war indicates that each attempted to act as a good citizen of the nation in which it was located (Vernon 1971). Such behavior might have been expected of Ford of Great Britain, but Ford of Germany also made contributions to the war effort on the German side.

The Ford subsidiary in Germany produced trucks for the military and, according to one account, even witnessed the bombing of its plant by aircraft manufactured by the parent firm. The total number of vehicles produced by Ford in Germany was modest (around 80,000), and levels of production in the Cologne vehicle assembly plant were half of prewar levels. According to Walter Hayes, a former Ford vice-chairman for Europe who is presently compiling a history of Ford in Europe, the quality of the trucks was not high.[1] Part of the reason was that before the war Ford of Germany had been mainly an assembly operation, relying on parts supplied from outside Germany itself. Early on, the major source of supplies had been the United States, but during the 1920s the subsidiary began to use parts supplied from Britain. During the 1930s, under pressure from the Nazi government, the firm began using parts supplied by non-Ford German suppliers, and after the conquest of Belgium and France it increasingly relied on parts supplied by Ford's Belgian and French subsidiaries. Workers in these subsidiaries were able to sabotage some shipments to the German subsidiary, and at least one high-level manager of Ford's Belgian subsidiary was active in the resistance movement.

Was the contribution of Ford of Germany to the German war effort reduced because the firm was playing the role of a fifth column or because of other factors? According to Hayes, "Ford Cologne was neither an effective collaborator nor a fifth columnist, but just a branch operation cut off from headquarters."[2] As we argue in the next section, a subsidiary cut off from its parent organization during time of war is likely not to be as effective a contributor to the war effort

---

1. Letter from Walter Hayes to John T. Eby, Corporate Strategy Staff, Ford Motor Company, 14 July 1989.
2. *Ibid.*

of the host nation as it would be if the links were maintained. And it is clear that those links will be broken if the host nation is at war with the home nation.

Could Ford have contributed more substantially to the German war effort? Germany's weaponry during World War II was technically good; indeed, in the view of some (but not all) military analysts, most German weaponry was superior to that of the Allies (see, e.g., Hastings 1984). Almost without question, however, Germany was somewhat behind the United States and Britain in the development of mass production techniques. In fact, one firm-specific advantage that had allowed Ford to enter Germany and compete against local automotive firms was its mass production technology (Dunning 1958, Wilkins 1970 and 1974). Had Ford been an integrated operation within Germany, it probably could have applied its technologies to help break wartime production bottlenecks (e.g., in the manufacture of trucks, of which the Germans were chronically short). One lesson, perhaps, is that nonintegrated assembly operations when separated from their parent organizations are of marginal value to a host nation's defense.

In any case, there is no indication that Ford in Germany acted as a fifth column on behalf of the Allies. Rather, the evidence suggests that Ford's German subsidiary behaved as a good if somewhat ineffectual local corporate citizen. Its affiliated operations in Belgium and France were another matter, but they, after all, were operated by local nationals in occupied territory. (For more information on the operations of Ford during World War II, see Wilkins and Hill 1964.)

In other cases, however, multinational enterprises have clearly used their subsidiaries to impair the military efforts of a host nation. There is evidence that US–based multinational oil companies actively worked with the US Department of State during the late 1930s and early 1940s to prevent Japan from building petroleum reserves. However, the early moves in this direction were initiated by certain of the oil companies themselves, to prevent the Japanese from discriminating against foreign-controlled petroleum companies and developing a locally controlled refining industry. In 1934, Stanvac, a joint venture between Standard Oil Company of New Jersey and SOCONY Vacuum Oil Company (today the Exxon and Mobil corporations, respectively), joined with Texaco and Royal Dutch–Shell (the latter then as now controlled jointly by Dutch and British interests) in an attempt to organize a boycott of shipments of US and Indonesian crude oil to Japanese-controlled refiners. The boycott failed when other oil companies failed to join in and the State Department indicated it would not support the boycott. Secretary of State Cordell Hull indicated at the time that he did not want a further deterioration in US–Japan relations (Hull 1948).

In 1935, during negotiations with their Japanese competitors, Stanvac and Texaco offered to give the Japanese research results on the hydrogenation process for coal gasification; these results could have had military implications.

The State Department knew of the offer but took no active steps to block it. Only in 1938, when US–Japanese relations had further deteriorated, did the State Department begin to apply pressure on the oil companies to stall Japan's development of its petroleum industry. Even so, sales of US refined oil product to Japan actually rose each year from 1933 to 1940, with the exception of 1938 (Wilkins 1974, Hull 1948, US House of Representatives Committee on Strategic and Military Affairs 1939, US Senate Special Committee Investigating Petroleum Resources 1946).

There also have been cases in which the conduct of multinationals has reduced the military preparedness of a nation even when there seems to have been no active attempt to do so. For example, beginning in 1929, Standard Oil of New Jersey entered into a series of agreements with the German chemical firm IG Farben, which resulted in Standard Oil stopping its efforts to develop a synthetic rubber and IG Farben stopping its efforts to gasify coal. The intent of the agreement was to reduce the potential for competition between the two firms within continental Europe and elsewhere. In short, it was a cartel agreement designed to keep each firm out of the other's markets as defined both by industry and by location (US Congress 1944, Haber 1971). As it happened, however, rubber was in short supply on the Allied side during World War II and petroleum products were scarce on the Axis side. The interfirm agreement thus probably damaged the war effort on both sides, although which was the net loser is difficult to say.

Conspiracy between multinationals and their home-country governments does not always hurt the host nation. When the home and the host nations are on friendly terms, such conspiracy may benefit the host. After the outbreak of hostilities between Germany and Great Britain in 1939, the United States at first remained neutral but favored the British in many ways. One of these was to encourage US–based multinationals to convert their British subsidiaries to the production of war-related goods. If this required something more than an arm's-length involvement of the parent organization in the management of the subsidiary, in a manner that could be considered inappropriate for nationals of a neutral nation, the US government simply looked the other way (Wilkins 1974). The British subsidiary of Ford made substantial contributions to the Allied war effort; for example, it produced over twice as many trucks as its German counterpart as well as 14,000 Bren gun carriers and tens of thousands of engines to be used in non-Ford vehicles and fighter planes. All of this production commenced well before the US entry into the war on 7 December 1941.

These examples provide evidence that the subsidiaries of multinationals may sometimes act as fifth columns in host nations on behalf of their home nations under circumstances of hostility between these nations, and that the most likely time for such action is the period immediately preceding the outbreak of war.

After war begins, links between the subsidiary and the parent are usually broken, although there might still be some communication by way of neutral nations. In all probability the subsidiary comes under direct control of the host government. Under these circumstances it is unlikely that the subsidiary could continue to act as a fifth column, although our example of Ford in World War II Europe indicates that even this is not invariably true: the seditious activities of its affiliates in German-occupied Belgium and France apparently had some effect.

These examples also show that a local subsidiary of a foreign-controlled multinational will not necessarily act as a fifth column even in circumstances leading to war. Numerous subsidiaries of US firms other than Ford operated in Germany during the 1930s, and we can find neither evidence that any of these attempted to restrain Germany's preparations for war nor evidence that the US government attempted to pressure them to do so. Had there been such pressure, it is not clear what would have come of it. By 1940 the management of most subsidiaries of US multinationals in continental Europe consisted almost entirely of nationals of the host countries.

The Effect of Breaking Parent-Subsidiary Links

Even if subsidiaries do not engage in overt fifth-column behavior, is there not some danger that severing the managerial links between parent and subsidiary will impair the latter's ability to produce goods and services needed in time of war? Again history provides no unequivocal answer, although there are examples where such disruption did impair the ability of the subsidiary to function. Ford of Germany, as we have already seen, did not function at its prewar levels during World War II after links with its parent and affiliated organizations were severed.

An example from earlier in this century is in some ways more relevant to present concerns. In the first decades of the century, multinational firms based in Germany controlled much of the technology associated with the then-infant chemical industry (Haber 1971). These technologies included the manufacture of high explosives. Following the United States' entry into World War I, the assets of US subsidiaries of the German chemical companies were sequestered under the Trading With the Enemy Act; after the war these assets were sold to US firms under provisions of the Treaty of Versailles. This treaty also called for German-held technologies to be transferred to the Allies. Several sources indicate that the US firms (principally Du Pont) were at first unable to utilize the technologies and eventually had to seek technical assistance in Germany (see, e.g., Zilg 1974).

Was the war effort substantially hurt by the evident fact that US and other Allied firms did not have access to German technologies before and during the war? One cannot help but surmise that it was, although there is scant surviving evidence on which to base a firm judgment. Any adverse effects were partly offset by the fact that German firms had licensed certain of their high-explosives-related technologies to British firms before the onset of the war. It is clear, however, that chemical firms in the Allied nations did not have access to many technologies that were available to the Germans.

The relevant question, however, is whether the Allies would have had access to the technologies had there never been any German direct investment in the chemical industry in Allied territory. For the answer to be yes, it would have been necessary for US or Allied firms to develop on their own technologies equivalent to those developed by the German firms. Would they have done so? It is far from certain. Thus, it is possible that Allied readiness for war would have been reduced, not enhanced, had there been no German direct investment in this industry.

One can interpret this case to support the contemporary argument that militarily vital technologies should be retained at home, in the hands of domestically owned firms, even at the price of some economic inefficiency. We discuss this issue further in the next section of this chapter. But the lesson from the case can also be read much more narrowly: the United States should never become dependent upon one foreign country that monopolizes a key technology, especially if that country could someday prove hostile. If a militarily vital technology were monopolized by a non–US firm based in such a nation, one policy response would be to require that firm, as a condition for access to the US market, to license the technology to US firms.

Another response could be actually to require direct investment in the United States as a condition for access to the US market. After all, if the United States depends upon the foreign firm for this technology, it is better to maximize rather than minimize the stake of that firm in the US market. Indeed, FDI could be one means of ensuring that the United States continues to have at least some access to the technology should relations with the firm's home nation go sour. For example, even though the United States was not able to exploit the full potential of the German-owned chemical plants seized during World War I, it is not by any means clear that the United States would have been better off without German direct investment in this industry. As we have just argued, the very opposite might have been true.

One further possibility, for very sensitive technologies that are under foreign control, would be to set as conditions of access to the US market both that FDI be "integrated" (i.e., that all inputs required for the operation, including R&D inputs, be located on US soil) and that the US subsidiary employ substantial numbers of US nationals in managerial and technical capacities. Such a condition would constitute a "performance requirement," something to which we are in general opposed. It is easy to invoke national security to support any number of requirements that in the end have more to do with protecting vested interests than with any real national security needs. However, in certain exceptional cases national security considerations could argue compellingly for such a requirement. The best solution, we feel, would be an international accord on direct investment that would generally forbid performance requirements but would contain an escape clause spelling out as explicitly as possible the circumstances under which national security could be invoked by a host nation to legitimize performance requirements. Chapters 6 and 7 discuss the issue of performance requirements further.

Safeguards Against Fifth-Column Activity

In time of war or events that could lead to war, is the United States adequately protected from fifth-column activities of US subsidiaries of firms controlled by enemy nationals or other conduct that could be detrimental to US security interests?

Emergency Powers

Assuming that the US government can identify potential fifth columns in wartime, it does have considerable powers to prevent them from taking actions that could be detrimental to the national security. The main powers reside with the President under the Trading With the Enemy Act (TWEA; its formal name is the Act of October 6, 1917). Under this act, in time of war the President can take any of a number of measures affecting transactions between subsidiaries of foreign-controlled multinationals and their parents. In particular, under section 5(b) of the act, the President may "investigate, regulate, direct and compel, nullify, void, prevent or prohibit, any acquisition, holding, withholding, use, transfer, withdrawal, transportation, importation or exportation of, or dealing in, or exercising any right, power, or privilege with respect to, or transactions involving, any property in which any foreign country or any national thereof has any interest. . . ."

This and other provisions of the act give the President very broad but quite ambiguous powers to act against foreign interests (see, e.g., Jackson 1977). It is clear that the original intent of Congress was to limit application of these provisions to entities controlled by nationals of countries with which the United States was at war. However, the original language of the TWEA also enabled its invocation whenever the President declared a national emergency. This was done on several occasions in peacetime, beginning with President Franklin D. Roosevelt's declaration of a national emergency in 1933. Then and later, provisions of the TWEA were used against foreign firms based in nations with which the United States was not at war or even in a state of hostility.

In 1976, concern about potential abuses of the TWEA prompted Congress to pass the International Emergency Economic Powers Act (IEEPA), which restricted somewhat the powers of the President to deal with a national emergency when the United States is not at war. Whereas under section 5(b) of the TWEA the President could sequester and (as the courts interpreted the law) take title to the US assets of enemy nationals during a national emergency as well as in time of war, under the IEEPA the President, in time of national emergency short of declared war, can seize foreign-owned assets but cannot take title to them. Thus, under such circumstances the President cannot permanently nationalize a US subsidiary of a foreign firm, although presumably (this power has not yet been tested) the President can put the subsidiary temporarily under US control.

Most of the other powers of the President to act against foreign-controlled entities in the United States are carried over from the TWEA into the IEEPA. These powers are quite extensive; for example, the President can block or regulate trade between foreign-controlled subsidiaries and their parent organizations. To invoke the IEEPA, the President must declare a national emergency under procedures of the National Emergencies Act of 1975. The national emergency expires automatically at the end of one year but can be extended by the President. The clear intent of Congress was that national emergencies would be rare events (see Carter 1988). However, the IEEPA has been invoked seven times under declared national emergencies since the passage of the IEEPA, including three times since 1985. In the views of some analysts, some of the invocations have bordered on the frivolous (see, e.g., Hufbauer and Schott 1983, Carter 1988).

Identifying Potential Fifth Columns

It has been asked whether in a declared national emergency the President could even identify those assets in the United States that are foreign-controlled. The United States does not require registration of FDI except for statistical purposes, and under present law the information collected is not open to officials outside of the relevant agencies, even in time of national emergency. Much has been made of this point, and in 1988 a bill was introduced in the House of Representatives that would have required registration of FDI in the United States and disclosure of certain information about its ownership. This bill, the Bryant amendment (named after its sponsor Representative John C. Bryant

[D-TX]), was not passed, but there is still some (apparently waning) sentiment within Congress to enact similar legislation.

From a national security perspective the argument over registration requirements for FDI is something of a red herring. What really matters is that relevant officials have knowledge of *all* foreign-controlled suppliers of goods and services important to the national security, whether those suppliers are US subsidiaries or the overseas operations of foreign firms. In other words, the Defense Department should also know the identity of its foreign sources that do *not* have US subsidiaries. Indeed, dependence upon an overseas source of supply for a militarily critical good is clearly a greater problem than dependence upon a domestic source of supply that is foreign-owned. The present state of the Defense Department's knowledge of who these suppliers are is not, according to some specialists we have consulted, as good as it might be. It has been recommended that the Defense Department take steps to improve its knowledge about which of its vendors and suppliers are ultimately foreign-controlled. In 1988, for example, the report of the Undersecretary of Defense for Acquisition and the report of the Defense Science Board both recommended that prime contractors be required to report on their foreign-sourced components.

We do not know how well these recommendations have been implemented. However, there is little to suggest that the holes in the Defense Department's knowledge principally involve foreign-controlled domestic suppliers. Rather, the holes seem to lie to a greater extent among firms actually located abroad that serve as subcontractors to domestic defense contractors.

Information on foreign-controlled firms that are direct contractors to the Pentagon should, in principle at least, be immediately available to relevant Defense Department officials. As is detailed in the next section, foreign-controlled firms that are direct contractors to the Defense Department are subject to special regulations that require disclosure of ownership. Thus, any gap in information involves not these direct defense contractors but foreign suppliers of so-called dual-use technologies to the direct contractors. (Dual-use technologies are those that are applied to both civilian and military goods.) We heartily agree that the Pentagon should know the identity of its major suppliers of dual-use technologies and related goods and services and should know whether these suppliers are under foreign control. However, this does not mean that every foreign subsidiary in the United States should be required to register with the Pentagon. Not all of these subsidiaries are suppliers of dual-use technologies, and not all foreign-controlled suppliers of these technologies are US subsidiaries of foreign firms. A task force within the Defense Department has been charged, *inter alia*, with looking into the matter of dependence on foreign sources of supply for defense goods.

Our discussion thus far has focused on foreign-controlled suppliers to the US military. Is there anything to fear from fifth-column-like action on the part of US subsidiaries of foreign firms that are not engaged in activities of military significance? We would argue that in general there is not. These subsidiaries do not have access to information that is sensitive from a security perspective, except perhaps to certain types of economic and commercial information that would be readily available to a foreign power through any of a number of alternative channels. If these subsidiaries nonetheless were deemed to pose a threat, could they be identified? We feel that they could: Emergency legislation could be passed allowing their identity to be obtained from the records of the Bureau of Economic Analysis.

We conclude that the US government in principle should have little problem in identifying potential fifth columns during time of actual war or circumstances leading to war, even without the imposition of new registration and reporting requirements for all foreign direct investors. Indeed, legislation targeted on gathering information about US subsidiaries controlled by foreign interests could miss the important point that the foreign sources on which the United States depends for militarily sensitive goods and technology are not limited to these subsidiaries. We do not claim that the information presently available to the Defense Department about these sources is adequate, and new legislation authorizing the Pentagon to obtain additional information about suppliers of dual-use technologies may prove necessary. But this is not the same as new registration and reporting requirements for foreign direct investors.

Other Aspects

Despite the extensive powers granted to the executive branch by the TWEA and the IEEPA, there are a number of aspects of the potential fifth-column problem that the US government can do little about. One is the fact that foreign-controlled subsidiaries invariably create domestic constituencies that could influence US policy in favor of the home nation of the subsidiary. One such constituency consists of US nationals employed by subsidiaries. The political influence of these constituencies could conceivably constrain the policy choices available to the US government in times of imminent conflict with that home nation. Actions taken by members of such constituencies need not be overtly hostile to national interests in order to put those interests in jeopardy—for example, workers employed by a foreign subsidiary might oppose government emergency action against their employer simply out of a desire to protect their jobs. We call this potential problem that of the "inadvertent fifth column."

It is truly difficult to assess the threat that the inadvertent fifth column poses. Our own feeling is that at present the threat is not great. One reason is that, in a national emergency, the President can seize the assets of a foreign-controlled subsidiary and protect the jobs of the affected workers. Assurances that their jobs would indeed be protected likely would dissuade the workers from taking actions contrary to the national interest. Another reason is that, although there is little question that European or Japanese direct investment creates at least a potential pro-European or pro-Japanese lobby in the United States, we do not think it probable that the home governments would try to use those lobbies in ways that are truly detrimental to US national security. Indeed, any such effort would likely provoke a counterreaction and generate strong antiforeign sentiment. Home governments are sensitive to this possibility.

A second potentially dangerous aspect of FDI that the US government can do little directly about is the impact on US defense capabilities if a US subsidiary's links with its parent organization are severed. That impact would be most severe if the United States depended upon this subsidiary as a major or sole source of supply for a militarily critical item. In most other circumstances the impact would likely not be great. To take an improbable example, if the United States were ever again to go to war with Japan, it would not greatly matter if Nissan's US truck facility, cut off from its parent, could not produce military vehicles efficiently; other suppliers could meet the need for such vehicles. Clearly, however, the United States must know what capabilities it will need in time of conflict and take steps to ensure that those capabilities are in place. This again implies that the United States should never be dependent upon a foreign nation, even through local subsidiaries of firms based in that nation, for a commodity or technology that that foreign nation is in a position to monopolize. We comment on this further later in this chapter and in Chapter 7.

One final aspect of the potential fifth column issue is that US subsidiaries controlled by foreign companies might leak information about technologies that national security dictates should remain in the United States. This matter is discussed in greater detail in the next section of this chapter; in general, however, we find that the United States is well placed to ensure that technological and other information vital to the national defense that originates within the United States itself is not placed in enemy hands by the managers of foreign-controlled subsidiaries. Access to truly secret information is limited to persons with appropriate security clearances, and these clearances generally are not given to non–US managers of foreign-controlled firms except under tightly controlled circumstances. Alas, the John Walker case, in which a spy ring made up of US citizens sold US Navy secrets to the Soviet Union, illustrates that there is no fail-safe way to protect such information when those who have clearance to receive it choose to work for the enemy. We simply note here that no foreign firm operating in the United States is known ever to have compromised US security on the scale of the Walker case.

FDI by Friendly Powers

The leakage issue concerns only technology developed in the United States. Today, however, the United States is only one of several nations capable of innovating technologies of military significance. Does this fact increase the vulnerability of the United States, and if so, what role do multinationals based in countries friendly to the United States play in the overall picture?

As table 5.1 showed, the vast bulk of FDI in the United States originates from foreign firms whose home countries are either military allies or other advanced democracies that are hard to conceive of as military adversaries. Thus, the main national security issue in practice is one of policy toward these friendly multinationals. Stated in extreme form the question is, To what extent should US policy assume that domestic US subsidiaries of friendly foreign investors are, for security purposes, just like domestically owned firms, and to what extent should it be assumed that they too are enemy agents? It is clear that policy should not swing to either of these extremes, but what intermediate assumption is the appropriate one? We address this question by asking two related ones:

- Are there activities in the United States that should never come under foreign control, even if the foreign investor in question is from a friendly nation? That is, are there activities so sensitive that it should be assumed that any foreign control creates a potential fifth column, in the broad sense in which we have defined it?

- Does foreign ownership by friendly nations threaten the US defense industrial base? That is, does it somehow reduce the resources on which the United States can rely to develop its defensive capability?

We shall address each of these questions in turn. But it is important first to note that proscribing foreign participation in defense activities and constructing safeguards against loss of militarily vital activities can reduce the ability of the United States to avail itself of foreign technologies of potential use in defense. Thus, we should ask not just whether US proscriptions and safeguards are sufficient, but whether any of them could have a chilling effect on foreigners who might be otherwise willing to bring into the United States technologies or activities that could be important to US security. This is not a trivial point; it would be sad and ironic if US policies designed to maintain the defense industrial base instead consigned the United States to technological inferiority by keeping advanced foreign technologies out.

Proscribing Foreign Control

We claim no expertise in determining which specific activities, if any, the national interest requires be performed by domestically controlled firms. It is clear, however, that both the US government and the general public regard it as essential that direct provision of certain key military supplies be done by such firms. Few Americans would feel comfortable if, for example, foreign interests gained control of one of the large defense-contracting aerospace firms such as General Dynamics, Lockheed, or Northrop. Yet no existing law or policy states explicitly which activities, or which firms, must for security reasons remain under domestic control.

Although there is no law specifically forbidding a foreign takeover of one of the major defense-contracting firms, the recently passed Exon-Florio amendment (discussed in the next chapter) does serve as a major deterrent to any such effort. It is safe to say that a foreign attempt to buy out Boeing would lead to an Exon-Florio investigation, and that by far the most probable outcome would be blockage of the takeover. Although the Exon-Florio amendment is the first US law that takes a step toward declaring that there are activities that the United States does not wish to see come under foreign control, it does nothing to indicate exactly what these activities are, and it establishes only very general grounds on which a foreign takeover of a US firm can be blocked.

Even so, the unwritten rule is that major firms engaged in large-scale defense contracting must be US–owned. There are exceptions to this generality, but these involve Canadian and British firms that have a long and proven record as suppliers to the Defense Department. This does not mean, of course, that all military contracting is restricted to US–owned firms. When foreign-owned firms provide military supplies, however, they do so under special and restrictive rules.

There has been some concern about whether the rules under which foreign firms can supply military hardware adequately protect military technologies necessary to US security. In fact, however, the rules are at least as strict and often stricter than those applying to domestic firms—it is arguable, therefore, that the *domestic* firms pose a greater security risk. Typically, a foreign-owned US subsidiary doing classified work must put greater distance between itself and its owners than must a domestically owned subsidiary. If one assumes that each set of owners is equally likely to be a source of leakage, it is then the domestically owned subsidiary that puts the nation at greater risk.

In the absence of an explicit understanding of exactly what defense-related activities should remain under domestic control, decisions with respect to maintenance of a domestically controlled industrial base tend to be made on an ad hoc basis. Although the United States under the Carter, Reagan, and Bush administrations has eschewed any formal government industrial policy, ad hoc decisions in this area can sum up to a *de facto* industrial policy that makes little sense as a whole (see, e.g., Magaziner and Reich 1982).

What criteria should determine whether a given activity should be placed on the must-maintain-domestic-control list? Obviously, one criterion would be military importance. That in turn depends both upon how important the output of that activity is to the waging of a military conflict and upon whether there are effective substitutes for that output. Thus, production of jet fighter airplanes is a very important military activity, whereas production of eggs is not. An army has to eat, but there are many substitutes for eggs; on the other hand there is no effective substitute for a state-of-the-art jet fighter.

Additional criteria would be the number of alternative sources of supply and the lead time required to develop new sources (see Moran 1989). A key characteristic of advanced jet fighters is that not just everyone can make them; in fact, the number of firms worldwide that can make advanced fighters or their key components is very small. It also requires a very long lead time for a firm that is new to military aviation to develop the capabilities needed to manufacture the most advanced jet aircraft. In contrast, although there is no military substitute for clothing manufactured from textiles—it would be impractical to send soldiers into the battlefield wearing furs—there are literally thousands of alternative suppliers, and it requires very little lead time for a new entrant to become established in this industry. Thus, we suspect that it would be considered vital that the capability to produce advanced jet fighters remain under domestic control, whereas we doubt that the same could be said for textiles and clothing.

Maintaining the Defense Industrial Base

There has been much talk recently about erosion of the US defense industrial base. Although the term means somewhat different things to different people, among national defense specialists there does seem to be a consensus that the "defense industrial base" consists largely of the high-technology industries. There are those who would include a number of low-technology industries in the definition, but this is a minority view held largely by spokespersons for particular low-technology industries that face foreign competition. Thus, what we are really addressing is whether FDI threatens to reduce the United States' strengths in the high-technology industries.

Having interviewed a number of defense specialists, we are convinced that there has been some erosion of the defense industrial base, especially within the electronics sector. But has inward FDI been a cause of this erosion or merely a symptom of it? We find that most specialists believe the latter. According to them, FDI is not a primary cause of the uncontestable decline of the once-dominant international position of domestically controlled US firms in electronics. Rather, US subsidiaries of foreign firms have displaced market share once held by domestically controlled firms in this sector because the domestic firms failed to keep pace in increasing efficiency and developing new product technology, not because the US subsidiaries behaved in a predatory manner.

Not all specialists agree with this assessment, to be sure. There are those who would point to the acquisition of small US high-technology firms by foreign investors as one way by which the United States has been stripped of the new technologies needed to maintain the competitiveness of its domestically controlled high-technology firms. The story usually told is one in which the foreign investor buys the firm, transfers the technology overseas, and leaves nothing but a hollowed-out shell.

Although most experts believe that some "hollowing out" has occurred, we find that only a minority believe that it is a leading cause of US decline in electronics or other sectors. However, there is a remarkable dearth of hard evidence on this subject. What evidence has been brought to bear on the issue is largely anecdotal, and we can find no systematic study bearing on the issue of hollowing out.

We will not explore in any depth the reasons for the erosion of the defense industrial base apart from FDI. One of the reasons that has been mentioned is the failure of domestic firms to maintain rates of capital expenditure needed to preserve a low-cost position in the production of such critical goods as semiconductor memory chips, which tend to be subject to dynamic scale economies (learning curves). Another reason cited is the failure of the United States to arrive at a consensus with respect to product standards, so that production runs can be made large enough to achieve these dynamic scale economies. Specialists indicate that the blame for this failure lies with both the industries themselves and the US government. In particular, there has been little effort within the Defense Department and other relevant agencies to set common product specifications. A third reason given is the government's failure to recognize that nonmilitary uses of high-technology goods today account for almost 95 percent of worldwide sales (we have in mind here the semiconductor industry)—a vastly different situation from that of 25 years ago. One consequence is that whereas a quarter of a century ago military applications tended to represent the leading edge of these technologies, today this leading edge most often lies with the nonmilitary applications.

If FDI is not the cause of the decline of US–controlled high-technology firms, is there any other basis for the claim that inward FDI has eroded the defense industrial base? We believe that there is.

If there were a clean dividing line between military and civilian technology, then the requirement that key defense activities remain in domestic hands would pose no particular problem: the United States could have a wholly domestic defense industrial base while allowing free right of establishment by foreigners everywhere else. Unfortunately, this is not the case. Not only are many important technologies dual-use technologies, developed for and applied to both civilian and military uses, but the output of goods for civilian uses is in some key sectors (e.g., electronics) much greater than that for military uses. This poses a potential problem. Consider the hypothetical but not entirely implausible scenario in which Japanese firms appear likely to dominate totally the production of civilian semiconductors in the United States, there are significant economies of scope arising from joint production of military and civilian semiconductors, and the US military considers it unwise to purchase key semiconductors from foreign-controlled suppliers. These products would thus fall into the category for which domestic control is deemed necessary, yet it would be unlikely that any domestic firm could produce state-of-the-art semiconductors solely for the defense market; in effect, the growth of foreign ownership would effectively have eroded the industrial base for defense. Unlike the purely economic effects considered in Chapter 3, this erosion would have nothing to do with loss of external economies. It results simply from the combination of dual-use technologies and a reliance on US–owned suppliers.

One answer to this problem would be to find a secure way to allow defense contracting with foreign-owned firms, as indeed most countries now do. Semiconductors simply would be taken off of the list of activities for which domestic control was deemed necessary. Under the current rules of Department of Defense contracting, however, a foreign-owned subsidiary can be a contractor only if it meets certain stringent requirements: either the subsidiary must be granted a special security arrangement (SSA), or its equity must be placed into a nonvoting trust. Under a nonvoting trust arrangement the foreign owners relinquish the voting rights of their equity in the subsidiary. The board of directors and top management of the subsidiary must also consist of US citizens. Effectively, then, the foreign owners of the subsidiary become passive investors. Virtually the only choice they have with respect to the subsidiary is whether to continue to own it. Since control is the essential objective and defining feature of FDI, this means that the foreign firm must in effect convert its direct investment into a portfolio investment in order to engage in US defense contracting. An SSA offers milder but still stringent criteria.

The preference for US–owned firms tends to limit the willingness of the Defense Department to employ foreign-owned firms as suppliers; in any case the restrictions placed on foreign firms tend to discourage these firms from seeking defense business. The result is that the defense industrial base can be said to be eroded to some extent when foreign firms acquire or replace US firms in activities that have military significance. This is a real issue and poses a problem for advocates of unrestricted FDI. But it also raises the issue of whether or not the rules under which foreign-controlled firms can participate in defense contracting should be revised. These rules were largely written at a time when the United States dominated the innovation of militarily significant technologies, including dual-use technologies, and were designed to keep sensitive technologies from leaking out of the United States. It is entirely possible now that they are doing as good a job at keeping important dual-use technologies out of the United States as at keeping US–developed technologies in.

A second issue arises when, in contrast, a foreign-owned firm participates in an important defense contract and, for some reason, the home government of the parent firm decides it wants the parent to pull out. Could this hurt the US defense effort?

An incident that occurred in 1983 illustrates both of these issues. Responding to the concerns of Socialist members of the Japanese parliament, the Japanese Ministry of International Trade and Industry (MITI) reportedly ordered Kyocera, a Japanese producer of high-technology ceramic products, not to participate in contracts to supply ceramic nose cones to the US Tomahawk missile program. Kyocera at that time was supplying nose cones through its US subsidiary Dexcel. Kyocera was also under pressure from the Defense Department to place the defense-related activities of Dexcel in a nonvoting trust. The outcome was that Dexcel was eventually sold to US interests. Kyocera is acknowledged to be among the most technologically advanced firms in the ceramics industry, and it can be argued that its withdrawal from this area of US defense contracting hurt the defense effort.

It is important, however, not to stress these issues unduly. First, the range of sectors in which dual-use technologies pose a problem is sometimes overstated, especially because national security is too often used as an excuse for special-interest politics. Numerous US industries have mounted campaigns against foreign competition in their domestic markets, claiming among other things that national security requires that domestic capacity in their industry be maintained at present levels. Trade policymakers have learned to look with a healthy skepticism on such claims, and they should cultivate a similar skepticism toward claims in the investment area. In fact, since cutoff of supply is even less likely when the suppliers are foreign-owned subsidiaries in the United States rather than foreign suppliers overseas, one should be more, not less, suspicious of national security arguments in such cases.

Second, to some degree the erosion of the US defense industrial base is a self-inflicted problem. Essentially, US military procurement is still governed by the assumption that US–based firms can supply all the necessary technology. Even under an optimistic prognosis for the US economy, however, Americans can expect from now on to live in a more symmetric world, in which foreign firms frequently have technology superior to anything available in the United States. In such a world an insistence on using only technologies developed by US firms will actually impair national security to the extent that it prevents the military from taking advantage of the best technology available.

Some Unresolved Issues

A number of issues related to foreign control of defense-related activities remain murky and must be studied further before useful policy recommendations can emerge. Among these issues are certain dangers that can arise from increased dependence on foreign-controlled firms for defense contracting, and whether hollowing out of US firms acquired by foreign interests poses a serious threat to national security.

We have suggested throughout this chapter that it will be necessary in the future for the United States to depend more, rather than less, on foreign sources for key dual-use technologies and that, if this is so, it is better to have domestic subsidiaries of the relevant firms do the work than to leave it to overseas operations. Two dangers to this policy suggest themselves, however. First, foreign firms cannot always be trusted to transfer their newest and best technologies to their US subsidiaries. Second, the subsidiaries themselves cannot always be trusted not to leak sensitive information gleaned in their defense-related work to their parent organizations, which in turn cannot always be trusted not to leak this information to hostile powers.

Whether, for example, Japanese multinational firms hold back their newest and best technologies from their US subsidiaries is a testable proposition, provided that the relevant firms cooperate. We believe that there is so much at stake that the relevant firms should be willing to cooperate, and it could be presumed that those unwilling to do so are indeed guilty of holding back. In Chapter 3 it was noted that the available evidence does not strongly support the "headquarters effect" hypothesis; this argues against the proposition that foreign parent firms withhold technology from their US subsidiaries. (Indeed, in many cases, the subsidiaries actually develop technologies that benefit the parent firms.) However, these conclusions were based on aggregated data. Evidence at a much more disaggregated level is needed.

Likewise, more needs to be known about whether US subsidiaries of foreign firms (or, indeed, foreign firms without such subsidiaries) actually maintain the secrecy of sensitive information made available to them. There clearly have been some cases where secrecy has been breached; incidents involving Toshiba are often mentioned in this regard. But are these incidents rare exceptions to a good record, or is there widespread leakage of sensitive information? An objective study of this issue would serve US policy interests.

In interviews we conducted with US government specialists in the area of defense contracting, we heard it alleged more than once that some foreign-owned contractors holding effective monopoly positions in the high-technology products they supplied to the US government had both withheld their best technology and inappropriately transferred technology to the Soviet Union. These reports, if true, provide evidence that concerns over increased US reliance on foreign-based defense suppliers are not unfounded. We do not think it wise for the United States to be at the mercy of any firm that monopolizes a product that is key to the defense effort, whether that firm is domestically controlled or foreign-controlled. Indeed the United States has antitrust laws on the books that are supposed to protect the US consumer from monopolies in any sector, whether of military relevance or not.

We have already noted that there is a divergence of opinion among specialists with respect to whether hollowing out poses a threat to US national security, and that there is a dearth of hard evidence to bring to bear on this subject. Study of the hollowing-out phenomenon therefore seems warranted. Indeed, proper administration of the Exon-Florio amendment, as discussed in Chapters 6 and 7, would seem to us to mandate that this study be accorded a high priority.

6

Current US Policy

The preceding chapters have surveyed the rising trend in foreign direct investment in the United States and analyzed some of its features. In Chapter 7 we draw on this analysis to evaluate a variety of recommendations for US policy regarding FDI. A few key principles underlie current US policy as it has evolved over several decades; those principles remain essentially in place despite significant changes as a result of the 1988 trade act. In this chapter we review present US policy toward FDI and compare it with the policies of other advanced nations.

Like most aspects of US policy, policy toward FDI needs to be understood at several levels. The first is the explicit policy enunciated and implemented by the federal government. The second is the implicit policy of the federal government toward foreign firms; this policy is evidenced in a variety of ways, not least by the precedents the government sets and the relationships it forms with other nations through its policy toward *outward* investment; these carry considerable weight because the United States is the world's largest home for multinationals as well as its largest host. Finally, an important part of policy that affects foreign firms operating in the United States is set not at the federal level but by states and localities. We therefore describe three kinds of policy: federal policy aimed directly at foreign firms, the important complementary policy toward US direct investment abroad, and policy made at the state and local level.

Federal Policy

Policy Toward Inward FDI

Philosophically, US policy toward foreign firms operating in the United States attempts to be neutral, without bias for or against foreign ownership of US productive assets. The general intention toward neutrality has been affirmed repeatedly by statements of recent administrations under both major political parties, notably in a 1977 declaration by the Carter administration and a 1983

95

statement by the Reagan administration. The 1983 statement was interpreted by some observers as more favorable to inward investment than the 1977 declaration, because it indicated that this investment was "welcome" if it came in response to market forces. However, since the United States never contemplated actually favoring foreign firms over domestic, this difference in language did not represent any change in the basic philosophy of neutrality.

A truly neutral policy toward FDI necessarily involves adherence to two principles. The first is "right of establishment": foreign firms should face no obstacles in creating or expanding US operations that are not also faced by domestic firms. The second is "national treatment": a foreign firm already operating in the United States should neither face greater burdens as a result of government action or policy than domestic firms nor receive special privileges that domestic firms do not. Broadly speaking, US policy toward foreign firms has been fairly close to neutral in this sense. The main deviations from neutrality come from a variety of special restrictions that are justified at least in principle on national security grounds.

Until 1988, federal restrictions on FDI applied essentially to those sectors subject to federal regulation. In a few federally regulated sectors FDI is simply proscribed. Many of these proscriptions were put in place during the late 19th and early 20th centuries. A history of these is contained in Wilkins (1989). These sectors include domestic air transport, production and utilization of nuclear energy, and most domestic maritime transport. In some other federally regulated sectors limitations are imposed on FDI. In broadcasting and telecommunications, for example, foreign-controlled enterprises may not own more than 20 percent of a company with a broadcasting or common-carrier license, except in cases where the Federal Communications Commission grants an exception. There are also certain specific ventures, such as the Communications Satellite Corporation (COMSAT), in which foreign participation is limited or proscribed.

In some sectors the principle of neutrality is superseded by that of reciprocity, whereby a foreign firm in the United States is accorded treatment equivalent to that which US firms receive in the firm's home country. Foreign or foreign-controlled companies cannot, for example, acquire rights-of-way for gas pipelines across federal lands or leases for mining certain minerals and fuels on those lands if the foreign investor's home country denies similar rights to US citizens or US–controlled corporations.

There are also some sectors of the US economy, such as hydroelectric power generation and fishing in certain areas, in which only certain legal forms of foreign ownership are allowed; for example, foreign-owned subsidiaries created under US law may be permitted whereas branches are proscribed. Foreign-owned firms participating in these sectors are also subject to US regulations such as the requirement that vessels flying the US flag be used.

Finally, although foreign-controlled domestic firms—and in some cases the foreign parents themselves—may participate in defense contracting work in the United States, these firms are subject to some special conditions (described in Chapter 5) if they work on classified projects.

There are some signs that the nascent US trend toward official promotion of certain high-technology sectors will involve a *de facto* policy of discrimination against foreign firms. Most conspicuously, Sematech, the federally supported research consortium in the semiconductor industry, includes no foreign-owned firms. In principle, Sematech's membership structure represents a choice on the part of the member firms rather than a federal policy of exclusion. In practice, however, the exclusion surely reflects the wishes of the US Department of Defense, which funds the consortium.

New Restrictive Powers: The Exon-Florio Amendment

The major recent change in federal policy toward FDI has been the extension of federal ability to restrict such investment in areas beyond the federally regulated sectors. The Omnibus Trade and Competitiveness Act of 1988 includes a provision that gives the President limited power to block mergers, acquisitions, or takeovers of US persons by foreign interests when such actions are deemed a threat to national security. This provision, section 721, is better known as the Exon-Florio amendment after its sponsors Senator J. James Exon [D-NE] and Representative James J. Florio [D-NJ].

The original version of the Exon-Florio amendment would have allowed blockage for a wider variety of reasons than national security narrowly defined, but at presidential insistence the so-called essential commerce clause of the measure was dropped. Under the version of the amendment that became law, the power to block a transaction can be exercised only if "the President finds that (1) there is credible evidence that leads the President to believe that the foreign interest exercising control might take action that threatens to impair the national security and (2) provisions of the law other than [the Exon-Florio amendment and the International Emergency Economic Powers Act]. . . do not in the President's judgement provide adequate and appropriate authority for the President to protect the national security. . . . "

The Exon-Florio amendment represents a significant extension of the blocking authority of the federal government. At least in principle, the possible grounds for blocking FDI are still narrowly based on national security, but some critics of the amendment argue that an administration inclined to restrict FDI could do so through a liberal interpretation of the national security clause. We postpone a critical examination of the Exon-Florio amendment until later in this chapter; here we offer only a summary of how the process now works.

The operating authority to implement Exon-Florio rests in the hands of the Committee on Foreign Investment in the United States (CFIUS), an interagency committee chaired by the Secretary of the Treasury and consisting of representatives from the departments of State, Defense, Commerce, and Justice as well as from the Office of Management and Budget, the Office of the US Trade Representative, and the Council of Economic Advisers. The CFIUS was originally established in the 1970s to monitor foreign investment in the United States, but until enactment of the Exon-Florio amendment it had no power to take any substantive action. The CFIUS undertakes investigations in cases where it sees fit and reports to the President either with a recommendation for or against blocking the transaction or, if no unanimous decision can be reached, with a statement setting forth the opposing views.

Under current procedures cases of potential concern can be notified to the CFIUS by any direct party to the transaction or by a CFIUS member.[1] Other parties (e.g., individual shareholders) can call a transaction to the attention of the CFIUS, but this does not constitute a formal notification. The decision to notify the CFIUS of a transaction is thus basically at the discretion of the relevant parties and certain government agencies. However, if the parties to the transaction fail to notify the CFIUS, and no CFIUS member makes a notification, the CFIUS can review the transaction at virtually any time it chooses; if the CFIUS then recommends divestment, and the President concurs, the divestment can be accomplished retroactively. For these reasons, parties to any transaction that might be deemed subject to review under Exon-Florio are being routinely advised by their legal counsel to notify the CFIUS voluntarily before closing the deal.

Under proposed regulations, five types of transactions are subject to the provisions of the amendment. First, proposed or completed transactions that result or could result in foreign control of a US person. Second, tender offers whereby a foreign person offers to buy a controlling interest in a US person. Third, proposed or completed acquisitions by US persons currently under foreign control of other US persons if the US person then acquired would come under foreign control. Fourth, proposed or completed acquisitions of US businesses by foreign persons (i.e., acquisitions where the business does not itself constitute a "US person," a circumstance that would arise if a US business were to sell an unincorporated division to a foreign company). And fifth, joint ventures that could result in foreign control over the business of a US person. "Greenfield" investments are not covered by Exon-Florio, nor are portfolio investments and certain others where the foreign investor does not have control

---

1. By "current procedures," we mean those established under proposed regulations issued on 14 July 1989 by the US Department of the Treasury. At the time of this writing these regulations remained subject to modification following a period of public commentary.

of a US business. Also, Exon-Florio does not apply to the sale to a foreign person of a US–owned business if that business is located entirely outside of the United States.

Upon notification, the CFIUS has 30 days to decide whether it will review the case. If it decides against review, the transaction is deemed not to be blockable for reasons of national security, and the matter is ended as far as the CFIUS is concerned (unless of course it should later become apparent that the decision was based upon falsified information or misrepresentation). If the CFIUS does decide to review the case, it has 45 days to recommend to the President whether the transaction should be blocked or, if no unanimous decision can be reached, to submit to the President a statement of opposing views. Upon receipt of the CFIUS's recommendation, the President must decide within 15 days whether or not to proceed with the block. The President has final authority on the matter; the CFIUS only recommends. However, it is not likely (at least under the present administration) that the President would block a takeover that the CFIUS found nonobjectionable.

Under the proposed regulations, the CFIUS takes a broad interpretation of what activities and industries are of relevance to the national security. No activity or industry is automatically excluded from the CFIUS's purview. The regulations do stress that some products or services have no special relation to the national security (e.g., toys, hotels, and food products), whereas others constitute "products or key technologies essential to the U.S. defense industrial base." However, the proposed regulations contain no rules or tests that can be used to determine unequivocally what products, services, or technologies fall into this category.

The first CFIUS investigation, in late 1988 and early 1989, was that of the proposed takeover of the silicon wafer division of Monsanto by Hüls AG, a German chemical firm. Monsanto was the last remaining US producer of these wafers apart from certain captive operations of vertically integrated US firms. According to press reports, some (but not all) members of the CFIUS felt that the takeover should be blocked to preserve independent US production of these products. It was also reported that the CFIUS negotiated with the transacting parties and that in the end Hüls agreed, as part of a *quid pro quo*, to maintain US production of silicon wafers and continue relevant research and development on US soil in return for CFIUS approval. CFIUS proceedings are not made public, and therefore we cannot verify these reports. Whatever actually happened, President Bush decided not to intervene in the merger.

At this writing, the CFIUS has received almost 100 notifications, which have led to four additional investigations. Of these, one resulted in a unanimous CFIUS decision against blockage (with concurrence by the President), and in two others the proposed acquisition was withdrawn. The withdrawals were in cases where the CFIUS likely would have recommended blockage of the deal as it was presented. In one of these the acquisition was restructured and the CFIUS renotified, and approval appears likely. The fourth investigation involved the acquisition of certain defense-related activities of Fairchild Semiconductor by the French high-technology firm Matra, and in late August, 1989 President Bush announced that he would take no action against this transaction.

Clearly, the actual role that the CFIUS will play in US policy toward FDI in the United States remains to be fully defined. One fear that has been expressed (primarily within the Washington legal community) is that the CFIUS will ultimately adopt a broader definition of national security concerns, so that potential foreign investors, recognizing the risk of intervention, will begin routinely to submit all proposed acquisitions to CFIUS for approval. If that should happen, the Exon-Florio amendment will have created a *de facto* screening agency for FDI. A natural further development would be for potential investors to offer to negotiate with the CFIUS over the details of their investment—as we have seen, this may have already begun to happen. If it does, then Exon-Florio has actually created a mechanism for imposing performance requirements as well (these are discussed later in this chapter).

This is an important point. Much discussion of policy toward FDI focuses on the possibility that future legislation might establish formal screening mechanisms and performance requirements. In fact the existing CFIUS structure could be used as the instrument of a highly interventionist policy *without* any further legislative action; all that would be needed would be a broad interpretation of CFIUS's mandate. So far this is not happening: in its limited actions to date the CFIUS has adhered to a fairly strict definition of national security. However, because the CFIUS's role is not yet fully defined, this could easily change.

Information Gathering

In addition to its authority to restrict FDI, the federal government plays a monitoring role. Part of that role is to collect rather detailed data pertaining to FDI in the United States. Foreign investors must report certain information to the Bureau of Economic Analysis (BEA) of the US Department of Commerce at regular intervals. The aggregated information is publicly reported as part of the BEA's mission to prepare and present information pertaining to the US balance of payments and the activities of foreign multinational firms operating in the United States. Information on individual companies is submitted to the BEA on a confidential basis and is available to only a limited number of persons mostly within the BEA. (Appendix A surveys the data collected by the BEA, to whom the data are available, and how the data are used.)

Information on certain types of foreign investor activity is collected by federal agencies other than the BEA, and some of this information is available to the public at the level of individual firms. For example, the US Department of Agriculture collects information on agricultural land owned by foreign persons. Certain specific information on individual foreign-owned depository institutions is gathered by the Federal Reserve and is available to the public on request. The International Trade Administration of the US Department of Commerce publishes lists of publicly announced foreign investments in the United States independently of the BEA. Also, the Internal Revenue Service extracts information on foreign investors from tax returns filed with the bureau, and certain aggregated series are made public.

A variety of reporting requirements set by the Securities and Exchange Commission (SEC) apply to at least some foreign investors. In general, a firm falls under these requirements if its securities are sold in interstate commerce, if it has over $1 million in assets, and if it either has more than 500 shareholders or its securities are listed on a registered national securities market. Not all foreign-controlled firms meet these requirements, and hence SEC reports are not available on many such firms. But many do, and even some foreign parent firms of US subsidiaries are subject to SEC reporting requirements.

A number of specialized federal regulatory agencies collect information on foreign- as well as domestically controlled firms falling within their specialty. Such agencies include the Federal Communications Commission, the Federal Power Commission, the Federal Maritime Administration, and other regulatory bodies.

Policy Toward Outward FDI

Policy toward inward FDI is inevitably intertwined with policy toward outward investment. The role of the United States as both the world's largest home and the world's largest host nation for multinational enterprises means that US policies play a particularly important role in shaping the rules of the international investment game.

US policy toward outward direct investment has two main components: policies concerning foreign nations that host US outward investment, and policies affecting the foreign operations and affiliates of US firms.

The basic US negotiating stance on outward FDI with respect to foreign nations is the counterpart of US policy toward inward investment. It is based on the idea that policy should be neutral regarding the nationality of a firm's owner. This means that foreign affiliates of US firms should be treated as domestic corporate residents of their host countries, with full right of establishment and national treatment.

US diplomatic efforts on behalf of right of establishment and national treatment of US firms abroad have taken several forms. The most important of these are US support for a series of efforts by the Organization for Economic Cooperation and Development (OECD) on behalf of liberalization of capital movements, the special agreements negotiated with Canada under the US–Canada Free Trade Agreement, and the ongoing efforts bearing on investment in the current Uruguay Round of trade negotiations under the auspices of the General Agreement on Tariffs and Trade.

The OECD Code on the Liberalization of Capital Movements is a 1961 legal instrument, revised in 1981, to which all OECD member nations adhere in principle. It in effect establishes neutrality toward foreign ownership as a norm. Although countries are given explicit escape clauses allowing both long-term restrictions ("reservations") and short-term blockages of foreign investment ("derogations"), these measures are treated as exceptions and must be publicly announced. A related document, the OECD Declaration on International Investment and Multinational Enterprise of 1976, is a largely hortatory measure that calls on member nations to offer foreign-owned enterprises national treatment and to report to the OECD Secretariat any deviations from this principle.

The US–Canada Free Trade Agreement was signed into law in late 1988. Despite its primary focus on trade it deals extensively with investment as well. It commits each nation to neutrality with respect to ownership by nationals of the other except in a few specified sectors, limits the extent to which Canada can screen acquisitions by US residents and firms (see the discussion of policies of other advanced nations below),[2] and calls for free repatriation of capital and earnings. The agreement also goes well beyond existing multilateral agreements in several important respects; most important of these are that both countries are precluded from imposing new performance requirements on investments that affect trade between the two countries, and that disagreements over investment policy can be brought under the general dispute-settlement mechanism that is part of the agreement.

Under the general dispute-settlement mechanism, the parties can agree to binding arbitration of disputes that cannot be settled through intergovernmental consultation procedures. This arbitration is not simply intergovernmental consultation continued in a different venue; in design, at least, it is more like an impartial judicial proceeding, in which individual parties to a dispute (or their representatives) can present their cases directly before an arbitration panel. In GATT dispute proceedings, in contrast, only government representatives can

---

2. There is considerable dispute among US business groups about the net effect of the agreement with Canada on the ultimate status of US firms there. On the one hand, the pact limits the extent of Canadian screening and performance requirements. On the other hand, it effectively accepts the principle that Canada may screen and regulate direct investment to some extent; some groups in the United States regard this as a significant concession.

directly participate in the settlement process. The US–Canada arrangement goes well beyond the GATT, not simply in extending the range of issues to which the rules of the game apply, but also by making the enforcement of these rules more of a judicial and less of a diplomatic procedure. These provisions move a considerable distance toward establishing for North America a set of explicit rules of the game on investment comparable to those that govern trade. Much more limited progress has been made in establishing multilateral standards for investment on a worldwide basis.

The United States has made it a priority in the Uruguay Round to include so-called trade-related investment measures (TRIMs) on the agenda. TRIMs are essentially performance requirements, that is, laws or policies adopted by a host-country government that are designed to affect the conduct of local subsidiaries of foreign-controlled firms. For example, governments sometimes impose "local content" requirements on foreign firms; that is, they require that the firm purchase a certain minimum percentage of their inputs from local vendors rather than import them. A similar requirement that might be imposed is for a minimum percentage of total value added of a product to be produced locally. Governments also often require that some minimum percentage of the total value of output be exported.

Performance requirements in some countries are linked to investment incentives. Typically, in order to qualify for a direct or indirect subsidy (offered as an inducement to get the investor to locate in the country), the foreign investor has to agree to abide by some such requirements. The BEA's 1982 benchmark survey of US direct investment abroad found that 28 percent of overseas affiliates of US firms reported having received one or more incentives to invest, whereas 7.6 percent reported being subject to at least one performance requirement.[3] Performance requirements are imposed most frequently by developing nations, although there have been numerous cases of performance requirements being imposed by industrialized nations (Moran and Pearson 1988).

The position of the US government in the Uruguay Round is that TRIMs represent distortions of trade that are contrary to the spirit of the GATT if not to the letter of the agreement. Largely at the behest of the United States, the trade ministers of the GATT member nations at their meeting in Montreal in December 1988 agreed to a work program within the Uruguay Round that directs negotiators to continue to examine the trade effects of TRIMs and the "relationship of the GATT articles to TRIMs," to consider where additional GATT measures might be necessary to discipline TRIMs and their trade effects,

---

3. This number seems very low. Officials at the BEA suggest that technical difficulties with the survey may have led to some confusion and a resulting understatement of the prevalence of performance requirements.

and to consider the "trade development effects" of TRIMs. This third item was put on the agenda largely at the insistence of the developing countries, which have indicated that they will resist any encroachment on their ability to control and regulate FDI and other activities of multinational firms.

The US government has identified 13 specific practices that it believes fall into the category of trade-distorting investment measures. There remains considerable disagreement among the negotiating countries over which of these measures, if any, should be disciplined through the GATT mechanism.

The US position on TRIMs was crafted at a time when the United States was primarily a home rather than a host country for direct investment. As the US host position increases, there will be a growing potential conflict between US interests. Indeed, we have already noted that the enhanced oversight powers created under the 1988 trade act have not only turned the CFIUS into a potential screening agency but also raise the possibility that the United States will begin to impose performance requirements itself.

It would seem a logical corollary of the US demand that US firms abroad be treated as residents that, in turn, the United States should allow those firms to behave as such—that is, the US government should relinquish any "extraterritorial" claims of control. Certainly what the United States expects of US affiliates of foreign firms operating within its borders is that they will not act as agents of their home-country governments. Unfortunately, the United States has not itself been consistent about this principle. It has on occasion attempted either to impose US regulations on foreign affiliates of US firms or to use those affiliates as instruments of US foreign policy. The most notable recent case was the Siberian pipeline dispute of the early 1980s, in which the US government attempted to prevent European subsidiaries of US firms from selling products or technologies to the Soviet Union, even to the extent of demanding that they break existing contracts. The United States eventually backed down, but the rules of the game were never really established. This episode is by no means the only example of efforts by the US government to use overseas subsidiaries of US firms as vehicles of foreign policy. Another major example involving France was detailed in Chapter 5.

The problems that the United States has encountered in establishing a consistent policy toward investment abroad carry an ambiguous message for the future of policy toward direct investment, now that the United States has become a major host nation. On the one hand, one might want to argue that the United States will henceforth have to do a better job of honoring its own expressed principles in order to receive the same treatment from foreign nations. On the other hand, it could be argued that the United States' own past behavior suggests that foreign firms will always be subject to pressure to serve home-country objectives, calling into question the principle of neutrality with respect to national ownership of firms.

State and Local Policies

Although some state and local governments in the United States have laws restricting the activities of foreign nationals (for example, New Hampshire allows mineral prospecting and mining only by US citizens), the ability of state and local governments to regulate foreign ownership is limited by the constitutional prohibition on restriction of interstate commerce. For example, if a foreign firm establishes a subsidiary in New York, that subsidiary is legally a resident of New York and cannot be discriminated against by Connecticut. As a result, there is not much economically important restriction of FDI at the state and local level. However, state and local policies remain an important issue in FDI because of two other areas of concern: provision of investment incentives and taxation.

Numerous states and localities attempt to lure major foreign investment projects with a variety of investment incentives. These incentives take various forms, including outright subsidies, various forms of tax relief, provision of infrastructure free of charge, and provision of land free of charge. Although in principle such investment incentives are available to all firms that might locate a facility within a locality, in practice they are often targeted toward specific undertakings that local authorities perceive to be likely generators of local benefits. Very large undertakings can find themselves the objects of bidding wars among local governments. For example, it was widely reported that at least three governments—the state governments of Ohio and Pennsylvania and the provincial government of Ontario—competed to attract the large Honda facility that eventually was located in Marysville, Ohio. Similar bidding wars involving other large foreign-controlled automotive facilities, as well as certain domestically owned operations, have been reported.

Since the incentives offered by local governments are normally contingent on a promise (which may be implicit) by the foreign firm to provide certain local benefits, state and local bidding for foreign firms may often amount to a *de facto* performance requirement of the kind that US diplomacy on FDI has attempted to limit. Competition among local governments may also lead to a kind of "prisoner's dilemma" that benefits foreign firms at US expense. That is, in order to prevent a new investment from being lured elsewhere, a state may feel compelled to offer the investor large incentives. All the states would be better off if they could agree among themselves never to offer such incentives. Nonetheless, if one state believed that other states were offering or were about to offer incentives, it would find it in its interest to offer them as well. Also, in the absence of an external means of enforcing an agreement not to offer incentives, some states would be tempted to violate the agreement, and this would trigger violations by other states. The investor, meanwhile, might be prepared to make the investment in the state even without the incentives, but will surely accept them if offered. The result is a transfer from the state's taxpayers to the investor, who sees the transfer as a pure windfall.

The other way in which local governments in effect make policy toward FDI is through their tax policy. The problem of taxing profits of firms that operate in many states has long been a difficult issue: it is probably meaningless and certainly impractical to ask, for example, what fraction of General Motors' profits is earned in Massachusetts as opposed to Connecticut. Most state governments have dealt with this problem by prorating the total profits of firms that operate in their state by a formula that takes account of the shares of in-state sales, payroll, and assets in the firm's US totals, and taxing the assigned share. Traditionally, however, this so-called three-factor formula stops at the US boundary: only US profits are taxed. Hence this formula is often called the "water's-edge unitary tax formula." A logical extension of the principle would be to apply a similar formula to the profits of a multinational firm, on the grounds that the attribution of profits to US operations is as elusive as attribution to an individual state within the United States. This extension is referred to as "worldwide unitary taxation."

Some states, including California, Florida, New York, Massachusetts, Colorado, Oregon, North Dakota, Montana, Utah, New Hampshire, Alaska, and Idaho have attempted to extend unitary taxation on a worldwide basis. California led the way by enacting worldwide unitary taxation during the 1960s. This led to widespread objections from firms that claimed it would impose high administrative costs and represented an interference by state governments with international commerce. This last argument was dealt a blow in 1983, when in *Container Corporation of America* v. *Franchise Tax Board* (103 S.Ct. 2933) the US Supreme Court ruled in favor of California. In spite of this loss, foreign-based multinational firms and in some cases their home governments began to lobby the federal and state governments intensively to repeal worldwide unitary taxation during the mid-1980s. As of this writing, California has a modified worldwide unitary tax that allows companies to elect whether to apply a three-factor "water's edge" formula or a worldwide three-factor formula. Firms electing the water's-edge formula must, however, pay an election fee. North Dakota and Montana have California-style systems, and Alaska retains a straight worldwide unitary system. The other states that have attempted worldwide unitary taxation no longer have such systems or proposals to create them.

In April 1989 the US Supreme Court agreed to hear a case that would reopen the issue of whether California had the right to tax multinational firm profits on a worldwide unitary basis. The argument of the plaintiff was that a state-imposed worldwide unitary tax is a violation of the constitutional proscription of state regulation of foreign commerce. On this same subject, the OECD Committee on International Investment and Multinational Enterprise (CIIME), of which the United States is a member, indicated in a 1985 report that worldwide unitary taxes "insofar as they do not impose a greater burden on foreign-controlled corporations than that on domestic-controlled corporations" do not violate national-treatment principles.

Both the incentives issue and the tax issue demonstrate a problem that may be increasingly important in the long run, as the United States adjusts to a large-scale foreign presence as a fact of life. Whatever the degree of federal commitment to neutrality of policy toward the nationality of a firm's owners, this neutrality may be offset or undermined by actions at the state and local level.

Comparisons With Other Nations

It is a common perception that the United States is much more open to FDI than other nations. Among the advanced nations, Japan, Canada, and France have legal machinery that in principle allows much more extensive screening of inward investment than anything currently possible under US law. A number of analysts (e.g., Glickman and Woodward 1989) argue that, because other governments have screening mechanisms, so should the United States. What these analysts miss, however, is that since the early 1980s this machinery has rarely been used, and recent studies by both the OECD and the US Treasury have concluded that there is little *de facto* difference among the advanced nations in their legal openness to inward FDI (OECD 1987, US Department of the Treasury 1988).

In Chapter 1 we cited evidence that both Canada and France are marked by high levels of foreign ownership in their economies, in spite of their history of restriction. In both countries, in fact, the screening mechanisms have largely been dismantled as a result of dissatisfaction with the results of screening. In Canada, what used to be the Foreign Investment Review Agency (FIRA) was in 1985 renamed "Investment Canada," and its mission was largely redefined away from critical screening of inward FDI and toward promoting Canada as a host nation for this investment. Also as noted in Chapter 1, Japan is an outlier: in spite of substantial liberalization of official policy toward inward investment since the 1970s, the foreign presence in Japan remains far below that in other advanced nations. Nor does this appear likely to change anytime soon. Although FDI flows into Japan have been much greater in the 1980s than previously, they remain small by comparison with flows into other advanced nations. For example, the direct investment flow into Japan in 1987, although a record high, was less than 3 percent as large as that into the United States in the same year.

We can find no evidence, however, that official screening of FDI is responsible for the low rate of such investment in Japan in recent years, except (perhaps) in a small number of defense-related industries. Thus, Japan's situation with regard to direct investment is similar to its situation with regard to international trade in goods and services: the market appears relatively free of overt legal barriers yet remains very hard for foreign firms to penetrate. The explanation of this paradox presumably rests on the same kinds of cultural and industrial-organization factors that are usually cited to explain Japan's trade patterns.

Evidently the differences between Japan and the other advanced nations will pose problems for any attempt to negotiate rules of the game for international investment, in the same way that they are a source of continual tension in trade policy. We return to these difficulties in our discussion of policy recommendations in Chapter 7.

The Japan issue aside, the policies of the advanced nations do differ markedly in another area, namely, the provision of investment incentives and performance requirements. Incentives tied to performance requirements are in general offered more freely in other nations than in the United States. For example, the United Kingdom, which is among the most open nations with respect to FDI, has not been averse to combining investment incentives with performance requirements. A case in point is the recently reported large British investment by Nissan Motors, in which the *quid pro quo* for investment incentives included both a local-content target and a commitment to export to continental Europe. Incentives and performance requirements are used by other European nations as well.

On the whole, the other industrial nations do not seem to differ greatly from the United States in their policies toward FDI per se. They certainly act less differently than a number of other writers on this subject have suggested (e.g., Glickman and Woodward 1989, Rohatyn 1988, Spencer 1988, Tolchin and Tolchin 1988). All of these authors suggest, for example, that the British government (which they cite as being among the most liberal of foreign governments with respect to policies toward inward FDI) can screen FDI on national security grounds. The truth is that in Great Britain the Department of Trade and Industry can refer mergers and acquisitions to the Monopolies and Mergers Commission, which can then recommend that the transaction be blocked for national security reasons. This authority in fact is strikingly similar to that under the Exon-Florio amendment in the United States, with the exception that the British procedure is more consistent with the principle of national treatment than is the US procedure: whereas Exon-Florio applies only to takeovers by foreign persons, in Britain the Monopolies and Mergers Commission can recommend blockages of mergers and acquisitions referred by the Department of Trade and Industry even when they involve purely British-owned firms, on grounds of national defense. In fact, the only recent case in which the commission actually recommended blockage on national security grounds involved a proposed merger between two British firms.

Where foreign governments do differ from US government practice is in their greater willingness to trade incentives for performance requirements. This, it can be argued, is more a matter of a greater willingness to engage in targeted industrial policy in general.

The US government maintains that investment incentives targeted toward "footloose" international direct investment and accompanying performance requirements act to distort the gains from this investment and from international trade as well. A major issue is whether the United States, either openly or through the back door (i.e., through Exon-Florio), will impose its own performance requirements. If it does, it will greatly weaken its case against other nations' practices.

Conclusions

US policy toward FDI is based on the general principle of neutrality, qualified by considerations of national security and marred by occasional lapses. Inward direct investment takes place with few restrictions, except in federally regulated sectors where the ostensible justification is national security. In this regard, the Exon-Florio amendment offers a wider scope for screening on the basis of national security, but we have yet to see fully how it will work in practice. In particular, we have yet to see the CFIUS recommend against a proposed merger or acquisition.

The United States expects and attempts to negotiate corresponding treatment of its own firms abroad but has weakened its position by occasionally asserting extraterritorial claims. This conflicts with the idea that foreign affiliates of US firms should be regarded as ordinary corporate citizens of their host countries. State and local governments also sometimes take actions that conflict with national policy. In all this, the United States is not very different from other advanced nations, all of which except Japan have long had a much larger foreign presence than the United States.

The question is whether the United States should now change its course. Does the upsurge of FDI that began in the mid-1970s mean that the United States should reconsider its policy of neutrality? We examine this matter in the next chapter.

7

Policy Alternatives

As we saw in Chapter 6, the federal government already has potentially quite extensive authority to screen and block foreign direct investment in the United States. In the federally regulated sectors of the economy there are significant restrictions on foreign participation, and the Exon-Florio amendment gives the President the ability to block foreign acquisitions and takeovers on national security grounds. Nevertheless, US policy remains in general terms at least as open to inward FDI as the policies of the other major industrialized countries.

Should the United States adopt a more restrictive, or at any rate more vigilant, policy toward FDI? The simple fact that such investment has been increasing is not by itself enough to justify such a conclusion. It would be justified only if we can conclude either that, absent special action, the increased foreign share of US assets and production will come about in such a way as to harm the United States, or that, absent special safeguards, foreign-owned firms will behave differently from domestic firms in such a way that US interests are harmed. If neither of these criteria is met, restrictions on foreign investment, including disclosure requirements that could act in effect as a disincentive, will generally tend to restrict the possibilities for mutually beneficial transactions, to the detriment of the United States as well as foreign investors.

The main conclusion of this study is that there is little evidence to support concerns about the negative effects of FDI in general. As we argued in Chapter 2, the growth of FDI in the United States does not represent a kind of artificial "fire sale" in which nonresidents are acquiring US assets at bargain prices. Instead, we are seeing for the most part a convergence toward levels of foreign control accepted as normal in other advanced countries; foreign firms enter the United States largely because of firm-specific advantages and other industrial-organization considerations rather than because of some financial distortion.

Equally important, foreign firms once in the United States do not generally behave as bad corporate citizens. Our analysis in Chapter 3 indicates that foreign-owned firms show no discernible tendency either to "keep the good jobs home" or to shift complex activities such as R&D out of the United States. Indeed, on average foreign firms pay about the same wages, generate about the same value added per worker, and engage in about the same amount of R&D as US firms in the same sectors.

The main exception to our general conclusion that foreign firms in the United States behave in a manner similar to domestic firms is the fact that foreign firms, and especially Japanese firms, do show an apparent tendency to obtain a substantially larger quantity of inputs abroad than do domestic firms in the same industry. Some of this difference may represent misclassifications (e.g., labeling as manufacturers foreign-owned firms that are primarily marketing subsidiaries) and similar problems. Some of the remaining difference may reflect a life-cycle effect: as new foreign affiliates mature they likely will increase the local content of their production. Nevertheless this tendency to import remains one real source of economic concern. We have argued that any trade and employment effects from the bias of foreign firms toward imported inputs have so far been minor, but the potential for future harmful effects remains, especially with respect to Japanese-owned firms.

The surge in FDI entering the United States in the 1980s has led to a number of proposals for changes in US policy in the direction of greater regulation. These proposals focus on four main types of restrictions:

- *Increased disclosure*: The argument is made that foreign firms should be required to make more disclosures about their activity than domestic firms.

- *Increased screening*: A farther-reaching proposal is that the United States extend its screening of FDI to evaluate new foreign acquisitions and establishments on general "national interest" grounds rather than simply on grounds of national security.

- *Reciprocity*: It has been proposed that the US government apply to foreign investment a legal standard based on the principle that a firm controlled by a parent company in another country would be subject to the same treatment that US–controlled firms receive in that country.

- *Performance requirements*: A number of foreign governments have demanded as a condition for allowing foreign investment, or for granting certain incentives, that investors meet certain performance goals that are considered to be in the local interest. Although there has not been vocal advocacy of such performance requirements at the US federal level to date, there is likely to be mounting pressure in the future for this form of regulation.

In this chapter we critically evaluate each of these proposals. We then put forward some proposals of our own with respect to future policy directions. These include limited steps that the United States should take unilaterally in the interest of national security. As will be apparent, however, we believe that the more constructive path leads to cooperation among governments on direct investment issues, and not to unilateral action on the part of any one government, including that of the United States.

Increasing Disclosure Requirements

Foreign firms operating in the United States are already required, for statistical purposes, to reveal fairly elaborate information about their operations to the Bureau of Economic Analysis of the US Department of Commerce. In addition, US subsidiaries of foreign firms submit detailed information to the Internal Revenue Service on their annual tax returns. As noted in Appendix A, this information is not made available on an individual-firm basis to the general public or even to Congress or other executive agencies. Instead the information is sequestered in the same way that proprietary information supplied by domestic firms is held for statistical purposes only.

A proposed amendment to the Omnibus Trade and Competitiveness Act of 1988 sponsored by Representative John C. Bryant (D-TX) would require that foreign investors in the United States register with the US government and provide information that, unlike the current BEA data, would be open to public scrutiny. The Bryant amendment was supported by labor unions that had experienced difficulty in obtaining financial information relevant to collective bargaining with foreign-controlled firms. The Reagan administration opposed the amendment, and it was dropped from the trade bill; however, a modified version, which would expand access to the information only to certain government officials, was reintroduced into legislation in 1989 as H.R. 5. Then–Speaker of the House Jim Wright, Jr. (D-TX), attempted to bring this bill to the House floor early in 1989 without passing it through the normal hearing process. The effort was withdrawn in March, however, and as of late 1989 the status of H.R. 5 remains uncertain. Other bills that would impose new or modified reporting and disclosure requirements on US affiliates of foreign firms also have been introduced.

We believe that passage of the Bryant amendment or similar legislation would be unwise and unnecessary, for the following reasons: First, it would largely duplicate an existing mandatory program for data collection that has generally worked quite well. Few serious policy analysts have found that the limitations on disclosure of BEA data present major problems in the use of the data. What problems exist instead involve the collection, presentation, and timeliness of the data. There are a number of ways in which collection and presentation of the BEA data could be improved to make them more useful for analytical purposes, and we offer a number of suggestions in Appendix A. These reforms, however, would be wholly administrative; they could be made within the context of the existing law and structure, without the need for a new mandatory reporting system such as the Bryant amendment would create. We note that a recent report on FDI in the Group of Five nations issued by the Royal Institute of International Affairs in London praises the BEA data on foreign investment in the United States as being more open and detailed than those published by other nations (see Julius and Thomsen 1988).

Second, since the United States already has relatively good information on FDI, the main consequence of the Bryant amendment would be to remove the screen of privacy. This could actually worsen the information by providing an incentive for misreporting. More broadly, by placing foreign firms at some strategic disadvantage, and perhaps by signaling an increased likelihood of future restrictions, the Bryant amendment could act to deter FDI. This is no doubt part of its intention; however, the conclusion of this study, as noted above, is that FDI is beneficial to the US economy and ought not to be especially discouraged.

In practice, it is not so clear whether the disclosure requirements under the Bryant amendment would put foreign-controlled firms at a disadvantage relative to their domestic competitors. On the one hand, domestically owned firms whose stocks are publicly traded must file annually the Securities and Exchange Commission's form 10-K, which is available for public scrutiny and contains more detailed financial and operating data than would have to be disclosed under the Bryant amendment. The 10-K filing requirement also holds for any foreign firm or US affiliate of a foreign firm whose common stock is listed on a US stock exchange or that meets certain other reporting requirements, but such cases are rare; for most foreign-owned firms with US operations there is no 10-K reporting requirement. On the other hand, there are a number of major domestically owned firms whose stock is not publicly traded (and which do not meet other requirements) and that therefore do not themselves file 10-K forms. Detailed financial and operating information often is not available to the public for such firms. The international asymmetries in reporting requirements probably have no greater (and no less) impact than this domestic asymmetry.

There is a case for arguing that information of this sort that is now available to the public for all firms listed on US stock exchanges should also be available for all nonlisted firms with operations in the United States exceeding a certain size. Like most economists, we believe that markets, including capital markets, work best when participants are well informed. But this reasoning surely would apply to domestically controlled "closely held" (nonlisted) firms as well as to foreign-controlled ones. There is no compelling reason why a nonlisted firm should be subject to reporting requirements simply because it is controlled by foreigners, when nonlisted US–controlled firms are not subject to similar requirements.

An extension of this argument is that there should be a set of minimal worldwide reporting and disclosure requirements for all firms above a certain size, including multinational firms. Such requirements, however, should not be set unilaterally by a nation to apply only to foreign-controlled firms. Indeed, because part of the desired information would be on activities of the parent organization, host-nation governments might not be able unilaterally to require such reporting. Rather, a set of minimum reporting requirements should be set as part of an international accord on investment. We return to this matter later in this chapter.

The most important point about the Bryant amendment and similar bills is that, although mild in their current form, they would mark a broad departure of US policy from neutrality regarding nationality of ownership. They would impose on all foreign-owned firms a set of reporting requirements purely because they are foreign.

Screening

Much stronger controls on foreign investment have been proposed in the literature but have not yet been introduced into legislation. Norman Glickman and Douglas Woodward (1989), New York investment banker Felix Rohatyn (1988), publisher Malcolm S. Forbes (1988), and popular columnist Jack Anderson (1989) are among those who have called for some form of generalized screening process under which foreign acquisitions and establishments of US businesses would be evaluated by a governmental body to determine the effects on national security and the economy. The screening agency presumably would have the power to block the proposed acquisition or establishment, or the President would have that power upon the recommendation of the screening agency.

National security concerns arising from FDI are already addressed by the Exon-Florio amendment (see Chapter 6), which charges a government body the Committee on Foreign Investment in the United States (CFIUS), with reviewing proposed foreign acquisitions for potential hazards to national security, and gives the President the power to block acquisitions deemed a threat to national security. With national security issues thus already covered, any further screening mechanism would necessarily focus on economic criteria. Also, implied in the power to block is the power to demand changes before granting acceptance, so screening by any government agency would inevitably imply the possibility of imposing performance requirements as well. We noted in Chapter 6 that Exon-Florio reviews of acquisitions of US firms by foreign investors may have already resulted in the *de facto* imposition of performance requirements.

Such a screening process would be comparable to those legally in place, but now rarely used to block investment, in Japan, France, and Canada. It would move US policy toward FDI completely away from the ideal of neutrality with respect to nationality of ownership, replacing it with a *de facto* industrial policy for foreign-controlled firms. It is not accidental that the majority of screening mechanisms of this type were implemented in those G-7 nations that in the 1960s and 1970s attempted to pursue strategies of industrial targeting, nor is it accidental that the use of these mechanisms to restrict direct investment has declined as these same nations have turned to more market-oriented economic strategies.

In evaluating the merits of proposed screening procedures, two questions immediately present themselves. First, to the extent that a supervisory role for the government is deemed necessary to prevent firms from making harmful investments, why should this oversight be restricted to foreign firms? Such discrimination against foreign firms might be justified if it were demonstrated that foreign-owned firms systematically behave differently from domestically owned firms in ways that are less than beneficial to the US economy. As we have seen, however, there is little evidence for this proposition.

Second, what are the screening criteria to be used? The problem of setting criteria is the same as that of setting general principles for interventionist industrial policy: Aside from a general proposition that free-market outcomes are innocent until proven guilty, there are no simple criteria for determining which privately undertaken activities are more desirable than others. Much popular discussion seems to presume that a professional bureaucracy could apply some set of accepted, objective criteria to the evaluation of proposed foreign investments. The fact is that no such criteria exist. In their absence, any US government screening process would either become highly politicized or turn into a largely irrelevant rubber stamp. Foreign experience with screening has shown both possibilities—often in sequence or even in alternation. The dangers and costs of a highly politicized screening agency, which would likely turn into an anticompetitive captive of special-interest groups, are apparent.

Although no legislation establishing a general screening authority for direct investment in the United States is likely to pass in the near future, we noted in Chapter 6 that the expanded role given to the CFIUS under the Exon-Florio amendment turns that interagency committee into a potential general screening authority; a broad interpretation of national security under this amendment could thus establish a *de facto* US policy of screening FDI even without new legislation. Thus, the issue of screening is not a hypothetical one.

To date, the CFIUS has defined national security quite narrowly and has taken seriously its charge to block an investment only if, in the words of the text of the Exon-Florio amendment itself, "there is credible evidence that leads the President to believe that the foreign interest exercising control might take action that threatens to impair the national security." This narrow interpretation should be maintained. In particular, the "essential commerce" clause of the early version of the Exon-Florio amendment should not be revived. To do so would indeed open the door to the amendment becoming the basis for full-blown screening.

Reciprocity

Prestowitz (1988), along with a few others, has proposed that FDI in the United States be subject to strict reciprocity. This means that foreign-controlled firms in the United States would be subject to the same treatment under US law that US–controlled firms receive in the home country of the ultimate beneficial owner of the foreign-controlled firm. For example, under such a policy US affiliates of Japanese financial firms could not act as primary dealers for US government bonds in the United States if Japanese affiliates of US financial firms were forbidden from playing the same role for Government of Japan bonds in Tokyo.

Interestingly, a recent major international dispute over reciprocity in treatment of direct investors actually arose not from US demands for equal treatment abroad but from foreign demands for equal treatment in the United States. During 1988 and early 1989 the European Commission floated proposals for a reciprocity standard to be applied to the operations of foreign-controlled banks in Europe. It appeared to the United States that, under such a standard, the operations of US banks in Europe would be fettered as a result of provisions in the US International Banking Act of 1978. Under this act, foreign-owned bank operations in the United States are subject to US restrictions on interstate banking which, although similar restrictions apply to domestic banks, are more stringent than those applied to US banks in Europe. Under pressure from the United States, the Commission indicated in the spring of 1989 that it would apply a national-treatment standard (under which foreign-controlled firms are not subject to requirements that do not apply to domestically controlled firms in like circumstances) rather than a reciprocity standard for US banks operating in Europe.

This example highlights a problem that would accompany adoption of a reciprocity standard for FDI in the United States. If reciprocity were applied literally and consistently on both sides, certain types of foreign investors could actually receive *more* favorable treatment under US law than would their domestically controlled competitors. To continue the example of the banking industry, either European-controlled banks operating in the United States would be freed from the constraints on their activities imposed by the International Banking Act, or US banks in Europe would not benefit from laws to come into effect in the context of "Europe 1992," which will liberalize banking activities that cross intra-EC borders. Likewise, under a strict interpretation of reciprocity, either European-owned banks in the United States would be exempt from the requirement under the Glass-Steagall Act that commercial and investment banking functions be kept separate, or US banks operating in Europe would not be granted the right, which other banks in Europe would have, to combine these functions.

Presumably, however, advocates of reciprocity have something different in mind: FDI in the United States would be subject to reciprocity only if US firms in the investors' home country are more regulated than these same firms are in the US home market; otherwise the foreign-controlled firm would be subject in the United States to something like national treatment.

It is clear that such selective reciprocity would discriminate against foreign-controlled firms, and that this discrimination violates the principle of neutrality with respect to nation of ownership that the United States has long advocated. Abandonment of this principle would be justifiable only if it were determined that the United States was both exceptionally open to foreign firms and was suffering losses as a result of its differential openness. In fact, neither condition appears to hold: other advanced nations are today similar to the United States with respect to their openness to foreign investment (with the possible exception of Japan), and, as noted above, we find no evidence that foreign firms operating in the United States (Japanese firms included) are predators on the US economy. It is therefore difficult to see why the United States should suddenly abandon a principle that it has long supported, especially given the still-massive US role as a direct investor in other countries.

Performance Requirements

Performance requirements are governmentally imposed stipulations that firms meet certain specified goals with respect to their operations within the government's jurisdiction. Such goals can include minimum local content or value added, employment goals, or trade goals (e.g., to export a certain percentage of output), among others. The United States differs from a number of other advanced nations in the absence of programs at the federal level that offer firms investment incentives in exchange for acceptance of performance requirements. (As noted in Chapter 6, however, individual states do offer such incentives.) The United States has also been working within the context of the Uruguay Round negotiations under the General Agreement on Tariffs and Trade (GATT) to limit the imposition of performance requirements and bring them under the purview of GATT regulations. Yet the United States in the recent past has actively considered imposition of performance requirements at the federal level, most notably through the local-content bill for automobiles that was introduced in the Congress during the early 1980s.

We would argue that continued US abstention from performance requirements is justified (with some exceptions in the national security area, discussed below) for several reasons. First, as US trade negotiators have often pointed out, performance requirements can amount to international trade distortions imposed by governments. In such cases, all of the arguments that can be marshaled against protectionism can be brought to bear: performance requirements are likely to lead to inefficient allocation of resources, and in particular they lead to the danger that resources will be allocated away from industries in which the nation has comparative advantage and toward industries in which local production is relatively inefficient. In the extreme, performance requirements could deter beneficial foreign investment.

To the extent that there is a case for performance requirements, it is a subset of the general case for industrial policy, and subject to the same problems, which are discussed above in the context of screening. There are no simple criteria that can be used to prescribe performance criteria that are actually in the public interest. As a result, efforts to impose performance requirements will inevitably become more of a political than an economic exercise.

We take particularly strong exception to the recommendation by Glickman and Woodward (1989) that state governments impose performance requirements on firms receiving investment incentives. The problem with performance requirements at the state level is that they would often have beggar-thy-neighbor effects, where the neighbor being beggared is more likely to be another state or region within the United States than a foreign nation. The real problem with state-level investment incentives is not the absence of offsetting performance requirements, but rather the inherent tendency of interstate competition to transfer rents from the United States to foreign firms. Performance requirements that make investment incentives appear a more attractive option for individual states would only aggravate this problem. Indeed, performance requirements could increase the willingness of state officials to expand investment incentives, thus magnifying the distortions. States would be well served if their power to grant investment incentives were simply abolished.

An additional reason to oppose state-level performance requirements is that, if successful, they would tend to undermine any US effort to achieve international rules to regulate trade-related investment measures (TRIMs). It is reasonable to hope that state-level requirements, if attempted, would ultimately be ruled in violation of the constitutional prohibition against state regulation of interstate commerce.

At the federal level, Prestowitz (1988) has called for performance requirements aimed specifically at Japanese firms. The essence of his argument is that, without coercion, Japanese investors are unlikely to take the steps necessary for the United States to realize the potential economic benefit from their investment. We regard Prestowitz's economic case as greatly overstated: Japanese firms do not show any tendency to keep high-value-added activities or R&D at home. They do tend to source heavily from outside the United States, and this tendency will become a source of tension if there is not a substantial shift to greater local content as the Japanese presence in the US economy grows. At present, however, the economic costs, if any, to the United States resulting from Japanese sourcing practices are quite small. Japanese private analysts claim, and their home government predicts, that Japanese firms will become much less distinctive in their import behavior as their investments mature (Nomura Research Institute 1989; Ministry of International Trade and Industry, forthcoming). If this does not happen, a "Japan problem" could eventually arise in US foreign direct investment policy. To call for an immediate radical shift in policy on this basis, however, would be premature.

Finally, even though no federal legislation imposing performance requirements appears likely to be passed in the near future, the same question arises that we have noted with respect to screening: will the CFIUS in effect become an agency that imposes performance requirements as well as screening? Commitments reported to have been requested by the CFIUS with respect to the Hüls AG takeover of the silicon wafer operations of Monsanto (discussed in Chapter 6 in the context of the Exon-Florio amendment) amount to performance requirements, albeit with a narrowly defined national security focus. As we argue later in this chapter, some performance requirements can indeed be justified on such grounds.

An Agenda for US Policy on FDI

The main thrust of this discussion of policy has been to arrive at a set of things that should *not* be done, even though they are popular in current discussion. We now proceed to an agenda of positive actions that the United States should take. This agenda can be divided into three parts: actions the US government should take to strengthen existing policies affecting foreign-controlled operations in the United States; actions that the United States should take with respect to these operations and national security; and actions that should be initiated on a multilateral basis.

Strengthening Existing Policies

Certain actions of foreign-controlled firms should be regulated as part of general US policy toward all business operations. For example, there undoubtedly have been foreign acquisitions of US enterprises that should have been subject to severe scrutiny, and very possibly should have been blocked, on antitrust grounds. The reason is not that the acquiring firms were foreign controlled, but rather that there exists a strong general economic case against monopolization. Otherwise put, there is a case for greater scrutiny and regulation of all mergers and acquisitions than we have seen in recent years, and such an increase would surely affect a number of foreign takeovers of US entities.

In other areas, however, there may be a case for further deregulation. For example, US restrictions on interstate banking effectively hamper interregional competition more than do the corresponding regulations in the European Community, and this is likely to remain a source of tension as European banks demand reciprocity. There is a good case for liberalization of US banking law. The case rests primarily on arguments that demonstrate banking deregulation to be in the US interest, although deregulation would also serve to defuse a potential source of international conflict.

FDI and National Security

The United States will also need to alter its ways of doing business so as to accommodate a larger share of foreign ownership in other sectors of the economy. The most important changes fall in the domain of defense. As we noted in Chapter 5, regulations affecting foreign-controlled firms involved in US defense contracting still presume that reliance on foreign-owned firms for technology is rare; this presumption is no longer true. It will almost surely become necessary to reform defense contracting so as to make better use of foreign-owned firms; the alternative, attempting to maintain a wholly US–owned defense industrial base, would be virtually impossible to achieve—even the Soviet Union now sources some strategically important items from abroad. The difficulties associated with maintaining a wholly domestic, wholly self-sufficient defense industrial base are likely to increase, as more nations outside the United States become sources of important new technologies.

The US Department of Defense already recognizes these realities and has taken considerable steps toward internationalizing its procurement during the past several years. This trend should continue, as it would be counterproductive to retreat from this path in the name of maintaining the national industrial base.

In this spirit, we question whether it is wise that consortia such as Sematech explicitly exclude participation by US subsidiaries of foreign-controlled firms. The purpose of these consortia is to develop and maintain certain technological capabilities within the United States. But the exclusion of foreign-controlled firms could do more to keep foreign-developed technology out of US hands than to contain any leakage of US–developed technologies to other nations. It might be better even from a narrow defense perspective to admit strong foreign competitors to the consortia than to exclude them, and to take other steps to ensure that their participation leads to a two-way exchange of technical know-how. One such measure is compulsory licensing, discussed below.

There are a number of other measures that the United States should take with respect to national security and FDI. Some go beyond the FDI issue per se and address the more general problem of international sourcing of goods and services required for the defense effort.

We indicated in Chapter 5 that the United States should explicitly identify what activities and technologies (especially dual-use technologies) should, in the interest of national security, be maintained under domestic ownership and control. The identification should be made by professionals with requisite technical qualifications and close knowledge of defense-related affairs.

What would be the criteria for inclusion on the list of activities that should remain under domestic control? We do not feel qualified to set precise criteria, much less to spell out what specific activities might appear on the list. Two general criteria were suggested in Chapter 5: the military importance of the activity (taking into account the availability of substitutes), and the number and diversity of potential suppliers.

What should happen once an activity or technology is placed on the list? If the activity or technology is already under domestic control, its presence on the list would signal to the CFIUS that a foreign takeover would be undesirable. If the firm or firms controlling the activity find themselves in financial difficulty, presence of the activity on the list might trigger consideration of government subsidy, although we hope that subsidization would only occur after investigation of other alternatives to put the activity on a firmer financial footing. If, on the other hand, the activity or technology is controlled by foreigners and there are no viable domestically controlled alternative suppliers, more drastic action might be warranted. We discuss below what that action might be.

We also argued in Chapter 5 that the United States should never become dependent upon a foreign-controlled monopoly for any good or service vital to the national defense. Indeed, the security of the United States should never depend upon any monopoly producer, whether foreign- or domestically controlled. Monopolization of a product or service is already illegal under the Sherman Antitrust Act, but it is questionable whether this law is strong enough to deal with all the sorts of monopolies that might arise in defense contracting. For example, in antitrust cases the courts have typically taken a broader view of what constitutes the "relevant market" than is appropriate for militarily critical goods. One option might be to amend the Sherman Act to narrow the definition of "monopolization" as it applies to goods or services listed as critical to the national defense (perhaps the same list of goods and services we proposed above). Monopolization might be defined for these purposes as a threshold market share held by one producer or by a family of producers under common control. We do not know exactly what the threshold level should be: it would surely be less than 100 percent but probably more than 25 percent. Whatever the threshold, defense-related activities would then be subject to more stringent antitrust provisions than non-defense-related ones. We emphasize that these criteria should apply to domestically controlled firms as well as foreign-controlled ones.

In some countries the relevant authorities already have the power to apply special criteria to antitrust cases involving national security. For example, in Great Britain the Monopolies and Mergers Commission has this power. Indeed, a recent proposed merger between two British firms was blocked by the commission precisely because the merger would have created a monopoly (within Great Britain) for the provision of certain defense-related systems.

If an activity or service (we define "service" to include the capability to develop a specific new technology) vital to the national defense is monopolized by a foreign supplier, what are the possible remedies?

As we suggested in Chapter 5, one remedy would be compulsory licensing of the capability to provide the good or service to a domestic producer. The US government clearly has the power to take intellectual property for its own use; compulsory licensing of this type is consistent with the Paris Convention so long as it is applied on a national-treatment basis. In fact, under 28 USC 1498 the Defense Department routinely uses patents or has them used by contractors. The patent holder is compensated under these circumstances, as is consistent with the Fifth Amendment to the US Constitution. Because many militarily important technologies fall into the dual-use category, compulsory licensing might be required as a precondition for participation in civilian markets as well as in military markets. A practical problem that arises is that although the government can legally work a patent that is held by a private party, the government cannot force the holder to surrender know-how that might be necessary to use the patent.

An alternative remedy that might in some cases be more cost-effective is mandatory foreign investment coupled with local-content requirements. These requirements could include provisions that R&D capabilities be maintained in laboratories and pilot plants located within the United States and that these facilities employ US nationals. Although such provisions would constitute performance requirements, which we generally oppose (see the discussion earlier in this chapter), they may at times be warranted in the interest of national security. Performance requirements of this sort, which would allow firms to maintain control of their intellectual properties, might well produce less international friction than compulsory licensing. Indeed, mandatory foreign investment would allow the innovative firm to maintain a large degree of managerial control over technologies that it considers proprietary, and this would be consistent with the principle embodied in US patent law that the innovator of a new technology should have a temporary monopoly right to exploit its commercial applications. At the same time, mandatory investment and performance requirements would ensure that the capability to deliver the goods needed by the military would be located on US soil.

We have already indicated that the United States should never become dependent upon a monopoly producer for a good or technology critical to the national defense. How do we reconcile this with our willingness to allow foreign investors to maintain monopoly control over certain technologies under our proposal for mandatory FDI? An easy reconciliation follows from the observation that the "no dependence" requirement applies only to certain very critical products and technologies. Thus, the only activities that would be subject to compulsory licensing would be those included in the list we proposed earlier in this section.

There are, however, cases where pragmatic considerations suggest the mandatory FDI alternative over compulsory licensing, even for activities that are included on the list. For example, a foreign firm that controls an important technology might choose to withdraw from the US market altogether rather than subject itself to compulsory licensing. In such a case, it might be preferable to allow that firm to operate on US soil while maintaining control over the technology rather than see the firm withdraw altogether. Under such circumstances, the United States might do well to encourage domestic entry into the activity.

Suppose, however, that a firm holding monopoly control of a militarily vital activity were headquartered in a country that at some point became hostile to the United States. What options would then be available? If the activity involved a US subsidiary, an extreme solution would be forced divestiture of the subsidiary to bring the activity under domestic control. However, as we pointed out in Chapter 5, the subsidiary likely would not be capable of producing the needed goods, or of producing them at peak efficiency, when cut off from the parent. Large federal subsidies might be required to resuscitate the operation. Forced spin-offs of activities critical to the national defense are not well advised if they are going to be dead on arrival. For this reason we consider forced divestiture a policy alternative that should be undertaken only under emergency conditions.

Under the International Emergency Economic Powers Act (IEEPA, discussed in Chapter 5), in a dire emergency short of war the US government can seize the assets of a foreign national but cannot take title to them. Exactly what this power implies for the takeover of a foreign-controlled subsidiary remains somewhat ambiguous. For instance, can the government seize such a subsidiary and place it under the control of a domestically controlled firm? Can the government itself temporarily manage the subsidiary as a state-controlled enterprise? These matters will require some clarification and perhaps modification of the IEEPA.

Overall, on pragmatic grounds we tend to favor mandatory local investment coupled with appropriate performance requirements as the remedy for foreign monopoly control of an activity vital to the national security. Such investment is overwhelmingly likely to originate in friendly nations, and our example of Ford in the United Kingdom (Chapter 5) shows that a subsidiary of a firm headquartered in a friendly nation can contribute greatly to the military needs of the host nation. In the event of a national emergency, however, it is highly desirable that the militarily vital activity actually be located on host-nation soil and that the activity be capable of standing on its own if cut off from its parent. For these reasons we believe that national security can constitute an acceptable reason for the imposition of strong performance requirements.

Another option when foreign-controlled firms monopolize the supply of a militarily vital technology is for the Defense Department to promote the entry of a domestic supplier into the market. How far such promotion should go is controversial. For example, to switch all procurement to an unproven "national champion" could result in dependence on an unreliable or technologically inferior supplier. On the other hand, to switch some procurement to a domestic entrant as a second source of supply could make sense. Clearly, the correct course of action will depend on the specifics of the case.

Multilateral Policy Actions

The rising role of foreign-owned firms in the United States raises the potential for future political conflict. Just as the United States has on occasion attempted to meet national objectives by means of extraterritorial application of its laws and policies to the overseas activities of US–headquartered firms, other governments might someday attempt to do the same with respect to the subsidiaries in the United States of firms based in their countries. There almost surely is no effective way that the United States could stop these efforts unilaterally through domestic laws or regulations without raising international tensions. What is needed instead is some sort of internationally agreed-upon rules regarding FDI, including a dispute-settlement mechanism through which deviations from these rules can be redressed.

The most fruitful approach would likely be an accord on investment and multinational enterprise among the world's largest industrial nations. To involve a larger number of nations in setting the rules would be both impractical and unnecessary: impractical because the potentially common goals among the major industrial nations with respect to FDI differ markedly from the goals of most developing nations, and hence agreement on a common set of rules would be close to impossible; and unnecessary because the vast bulk of FDI at present takes place among a relatively small number of industrially advanced nations. Nonetheless, it should be made possible for nations outside the core group eventually to sign the FDI accord as well; some less-developed countries, and notably some of the newly industrializing countries, might be willing to do so.

There would be some procedural problems to be worked out with any such accord. For example, the European nations might have to enter the agreement via the European Community. If so, the interests of some of the smaller and poorer members of the Community would have to be taken into account. An accord on FDI among the advanced industrial nations—whether just the G-7 or a somewhat larger group that would include all of the EC nations—would, however, be highly desirable.

Such an accord is more feasible now than at any time in the recent past, for a number of reasons: First, the United States, for the first time in this century, is developing a large and visible foreign-controlled sector within its domestic economy; therefore, for the first time the United States is being compelled to consider the implications of its own policies with respect to outward FDI upon inward FDI and vice versa. Second, under the aegis of Europe 1992, the European nations are moving toward common policies to govern both intra-European direct investment and direct investment across Community borders in both directions. Third, the US–Canada Free Trade Agreement has created a precedent for a dispute-settlement procedure governing investment. Fourth, Japan has exhibited at least a rhetorical commitment to more-open investment policies. None of these factors ensures that an effective accord could actually be reached, yet none of them even existed ten years ago. We have noted already that among the major industrial countries there is now more convergence of national policies regarding FDI than at any time in the recent past. In other words, if the time for a new international initiative in this domain is not now, it is not far off.

It is possible to sketch out some of the elements such an accord should include. One is some formal declaration of the basic rights and responsibilities of home nations, host nations, and multinational enterprises. This should not be a long list. Host-nation responsibilities would include the granting of right of establishment and national treatment to local subsidiaries of foreign parentage. Acceptable deviations from these principles would also have to be enumerated.

Home-nation rights and responsibilities should also be spelled out. In general, home nations should have the right to take appropriate action to protect the domestic property rights of their citizens, including locally based multinational corporations, and to protect their citizens' rights with respect to property held in foreign nations. This right must, however, be delimited. It is not appropriate for a home government to attempt to use the property rights of its citizens who own overseas subsidiaries as vehicles for extending home-nation policies or laws abroad, especially when these conflict with host-country policies or laws. Thus, for example, it would be appropriate for a home government to attempt to guarantee that one of its multinational firms facing expropriation of properties abroad was treated in a nondiscriminatory manner. But it would not be appropriate for the home government to insist that its own standards be applied to the expropriation process.

What this does and does not imply for the conduct of multinational firms and their home nations can be illustrated by a further example. Suppose that a US subsidiary of a Japanese firm decided to hire a former high-level US official to represent it in its dealings with the federal government. So long as a US firm engaged in comparable business could legally hire the same official for the same purposes, there would be no problem with respect to national treatment. Indeed any US law specifically forbidding such hiring by foreign-controlled firms would be a violation of the national-treatment principle, and the Japanese government could legitimately complain that Japanese investors were subject to discriminatory procedures. However, if the subsidiary were to respond to parent-company orders that were in turn a response to instructions from the Japanese Ministry of International Trade and Industry (MITI), this would be an abuse of home-country rights as defined above. Direct countermeasures by the US government would then not necessarily violate the principle of national treatment, although a better US response might be an appeal to the dispute-settlement mechanism outlined below.

Responsibilities of multinational firms would include a commitment not to compel their overseas subsidiaries to disobey the laws of the jurisdictions in which they are located. An important extension of this principle, consistent with the home-nation government responsibilities outlined above, would be to ensure that if the subsidiary's efforts to obey local laws come into conflict with directives from the parent company (perhaps to comply with laws or policies of the home government), obeying the local laws shall take precedence.

Other responsibilities of firms under an international accord could include compliance with requirements for public disclosure of certain current financial and operating information. In other words, there is a case for something like a Bryant amendment at the international level. However, any such provision should not force multinational firms to disclose publicly more information than is required of locally controlled firms operating in the same locality and industry. One option would be a set of common standards for disclosure and reporting that would apply to all business enterprises exceeding a specified size threshold.

The accord should include restrictions on the use of performance requirements. The US–Canada Free Trade Agreement provides a model for such restrictions. Under this agreement, new performance requirements that affect international trade are proscribed, whereas certain others are grandfathered. A multilateral extension of this proscription would be desirable, and indeed we see an accord among a limited group of nations as a more practical basis for such a proscription than the current TRIMs discussions within the Uruguay Round. A useful approach here would be, first, to develop a list of practices that are deemed to distort international commerce and therefore are to be banned or avoided; second, to develop a list of specific practices now in place that are to be grandfathered, and another list of practices now in place that are to be phased out; third, to develop a list of acceptable categories of performance requirements (we have in mind requirements that are deemed necessary for reasons of national security, as discussed earlier in this chapter, but we cannot exclude that other acceptable categories may emerge); and fourth, to establish a mechanism for monitoring and regulating the use of these requirements.

A further desirable extension would be some limitation on the use of investment incentives. If such a limitation were to be implemented, the United States would have to ensure that the individual states comply. As we have suggested, limitation of these incentives would be in the states' own best overall interest.

There are numerous domains in which problems posed by the existence of multinational corporations would be best resolved by consultation and agreement among the relevant national governmental agencies. Examples include questions of taxation, antitrust and control of restrictive business practices, pollution and environmental standards, security export control, product safety and liability standards, and other areas where public regulation of private enterprise is deemed necessary. It is entirely possible that, in different domains, different institutional mechanisms will be brought to bear. For example, jurisprudential mechanisms, including perhaps mechanisms that have not yet been created (e.g., an international tribunal to adjudicate cases involving anticompetitive practices), might well figure heavily in antitrust matters, whereas in the domain of taxation the primary mechanism would remain national tax authorities whose functions are linked via a network of tax treaties.

Thus, we do not in general believe that our proposed accord should initially include specific "codes" to deal with these domains. Rather, it should provide a framework within which relevant national authorities might consult and, where appropriate, cooperate among themselves. Modes of cooperation might vary from domain to domain. For example, in one domain explicit rules might be embodied in the form of a code, whereas in another the cooperation might be limited to formal avenues of consultation.

To some degree the Organization for Economic Cooperation and Development (OECD) already provides such a framework. The OECD has, for example, been very successful in fostering a series of treaties bearing on the taxation of multinational enterprises and mechanisms of cooperation among national tax authorities to administer the treaties. The existing framework is, however, very informal, and its effectiveness is spotty. What is needed is an enlargement of this framework.

An essential ingredient of such an enlargement is an effective dispute-settlement mechanism. Here the US–Canada Free Trade Agreement again shows the way. The dispute-settlement mechanism for trade established under this agreement is stronger than other existing mechanisms (e.g., that of the GATT) in two respects: First, disputes that cannot be settled through intergovernmental consultation can be subject to binding arbitration (albeit only with the consent of the disputing governments); second, private parties and relevant national authorities involved in a dispute have the right to appear before the arbitration panel. These provisions should be carried forward into our proposed international accord on investment. Indeed, they should be strengthened, and disputes that cannot be settled through intergovernmental consultation should be subject to *mandatory* binding arbitration.

In addition, the US–Canada agreement is stronger than the GATT in one other important respect: The United States participates in the GATT by virtue of an executive order rather than on the basis of congressional legislation. As a consequence, the US Congress has never felt bound by the provisions of the GATT, including the outcomes of its dispute-settlement procedures. The US–Canada agreement, in contrast, was ratified by Congress, and its provisions are therefore US law, not simply executive commitments. We would hope that our proposed accord would also have the formal approval of Congress.

For this approval to come about, both the Congress and the President must recognize that there is substantial potential for nations to harm one another through unilateral actions in the domain of international investment. Such harm can be prevented only by international rules to govern international investment and home- and host-nations' policies affecting that investment.

Conclusions

The role of foreign-owned firms in the US economy has increased sharply in the 1980s and is likely to continue to increase. We hope that we have shown satisfactorily that there is nothing sinister about this increased role, and that indeed its general economic effect is beneficial. Thus, there is no need from an economic perspective for new unilateral laws or policies specifically targeted toward greater regulation of foreign-controlled activities in the United States. This does not imply that in a fast-changing world there is no need for a continual rethinking of the ideas upon which policies rest. There is, and in some cases the outcome might be more regulation affecting FDI (e.g., stronger enforcement of certain of the antitrust laws) and in other cases less (e.g., in banking and defense).

The rapid growth of FDI in the United States will, of course, continue to generate political tensions. In particular, it seems quite possible that the United States will face a "Japan problem" in its international investment policy, just as it does in its international trade policy. Japan remains an outlier both in terms of penetration of its economy by foreign firms and in terms of the behavior of Japanese-based firms in the United States.

If anything, Japan is even more of an outlier in terms of the low level of foreign control of its economy than it is in terms of its low propensity to import manufactured goods. As in the case of trade in manufactures, however, Japan's difference from other advanced nations in this respect seems to owe little to differences in current government policy, which is roughly as open to direct investment as that in other advanced nations. Instead, there appear to be differences in the structure of Japan's economy that make it difficult for foreign firms to penetrate. Although there are reasons to hope that Japan will eventually become increasingly open both to imports and to direct investment, for a long time to come Japan's outlier status will be a source of tension.

To this must be added the apparent difference in import behavior exhibited by Japanese firms in the United States. It is important not to overstate this difference and accuse Japanese firms of antisocial behavior. In most respects Japanese firms in the United States look quite normal. For example, the widespread belief that Japanese firms keep high value-added activities or R&D at home is not borne out by the data. Japanese firms in the United States do, however, import considerably more per employee even in comparable activities than do other foreign direct investors, and much more than do domestically owned firms. Japanese firms and Japanese government officials argue that this is a transitional phenomenon reflecting the newness of their direct investment here. We hope that this turns out to be the case; otherwise a rethinking of US openness to direct investment will become difficult to avoid.

It is important, however, to reiterate that on economic grounds the case in favor of an open policy toward FDI, including investment from Japan, remains strong. Even where the case against direct investment is strongest, on the import issue, the maximum possible cost is small, and it is quite possible that there is in fact a gain, because direct investment may displace imports. In our view, the evidence does not shake the presumption that FDI in general makes a significant positive contribution to the US economy.

Indeed, the major threat to US welfare comes not from the growing foreign presence but from the potential for an "investment war" in which governments attempt unilaterally to capture greater benefits from foreign investment through such measures as performance requirements, or attempt to use multinationals headquartered in their territories to further their own foreign policy interests at the possible expense of nations that are hosts to subsidiaries of these enterprises. (For an early delineation of the dangers of investment wars, see Bergsten 1974.)

Cooperative action is essential if investment wars are to be avoided. The United States must avoid hysteria; like other advanced nations that have experienced waves of inward direct investment, it will eventually realize that on the whole the process is highly beneficial. But other players, especially Japan, must also make efforts to ensure that their own behavior is conducive to a liberal world climate for direct investment. And we should take seriously the possibility that an explicit multilateral agreement on direct investment can be reached. Like the GATT, such an agreement will not solve all our problems, but also like the GATT, it could do us all a lot of good.

Appendices

Appendix A   US Government Data on Foreign Direct Investment

One of the more contentious issues in the debate over foreign direct investment in the United States is the adequacy of data on this investment collected by the US government. Several federal agencies collect data on various aspects of FDI, but the Bureau of Economic Analysis (BEA), an agency of the US Department of Commerce, has the major role. In this appendix we survey the nature of the information the BEA gathers and assess its adequacy for policy analysis.

The BEA is the federal agency responsible for the preparation of the US national income and product accounts, the balance of payments accounts, and a number of other important data series. The BEA publishes these data in its monthly *Survey of Current Business* and in greater detail in separate volumes. For most of its data the BEA relies on information supplied by other government bureaus and agencies; relatively few data are collected by the BEA itself directly from private-sector sources. However, among the data that the BEA does collect directly are those on inward and outward FDI.

The BEA is a small agency by federal government standards, with a total 1988 budget of $32.1 million. The BEA's budget was reduced sharply during the Reagan years. By one estimate, the cut amounted to 8 percent annually in real terms from 1981 to 1988. In 1988 the total staff of the BEA consisted of 391 persons, compared to 455 in 1980.

Nature and Collection of BEA Data

The BEA's collection of data on inward FDI is conducted under the authority of the International Investment and Trade in Services Survey Act. This law was passed in 1976 largely in response to congressional fears that investors from member nations of the Organization of Petroleum Exporting Countries (OPEC) were acquiring too large a stake in the US economy. The act was amended in 1984 to include data on services. The BEA collected data on the activities of US affiliates of foreign companies before the passage of the Survey Act, but the act increased the scope of the information gathered.

Compliance with the BEA surveys of US affiliates of foreign companies is mandatory; that is, the affiliates are required by law to furnish the requested information. However, the BEA treats records for individual affiliates and their parent companies as confidential. Access is restricted to BEA staff, certain consultants and contractors to the BEA, and a limited number of other government officials specifically designated to perform certain functions under the Survey Act. Persons with access to the records may not disclose to the public information that would identify the company furnishing the information. The records are closed to Congress and to other executive officials not specifically granted access under the act. The data may be used for statistical and analytical purposes only; in particular, they may not be used for purposes of investigation or regulation or to determine tax liability. For reporting purposes, a US affiliate of a foreign company is defined as a US business enterprise in which a foreign person (actual or corporate) owns, directly or indirectly, at least 10 percent of the voting equity (or the equivalent if the enterprise is unincorporated). Under the law, it is the responsibility of any affiliate meeting these criteria to identify itself to the BEA and to provide the required information.

The BEA collects and publishes two types of data on FDI: balance of payments data and financial and operating data. Balance of payments information gathered by the BEA includes data on the value of current holdings (positions) of foreign direct investors as well as transactions between US affiliates and their foreign parents. This information is needed to calculate the US balance of payments and the national income and product accounts as well as the international investment position of the United States. The transactions information includes equity and interfirm debt flows between the affiliates and their parents; income flows, royalties, and license fees; and other services transactions. Information on the international investment position of the United States includes the stocks of foreign parents' equity in and their net outstanding loans to their US affiliates. Detailed tabulations are published by industry of US affiliate and by country of foreign parent.

Financial and operating data collected by the BEA cover the overall financial structure and operations of US affiliates of foreign firms. Much of this information consists of general income and balance sheet information. Certain items of specific interest that might not be carried on the firms' income statements and balance sheets are also collected, such as the value of affiliates' US merchandise exports and imports; property, plant, and equipment expenditures; number of workers employed and their compensation; and research and development expenditures. Detailed tabulations are published by industry of US affiliate, by country of ultimate beneficial owner, and (for selected items) by state.

It is important to distinguish clearly between the balance of payments data and the financial and operating data. We have seen critics of the BEA data confuse, for example, total assets of US affiliates of foreign firms with the total stock of FDI in the United States on a balance of payments basis. The latter consists essentially of the net equity and interfirm debt claims of foreign parents on their US affiliates and is therefore quite different from total assets. It is entirely possible (and indeed likely) that these two series will grow at different rates. For example, if a large foreign parent firm increases its equity share in its US affiliate from 50 to 100 percent, then all else being equal, the total stock of FDI in the United States will grow by the amount of the additional equity, yet the transaction will have no effect on the total assets of US affiliates of foreign firms.

The BEA collects its data by three means: the comprehensive but relatively infrequent benchmark survey, yearly and quarterly sample surveys, and a yearly survey of US businesses newly acquired or established by foreign direct investors.

The BEA considers the benchmark survey to be the foundation of its reporting system. Normally this survey is conducted at least once every five years. The most recent surveys, however, were those for 1987 and 1980. The seven-year lag in this case was exceptional; its purpose was to have the benchmark survey coincide with the economic censuses performed by the Bureau of the Census so that data from the two agencies could be related and combined.

The benchmark survey is more comprehensive than the other surveys in terms of both the amount of information gathered from each reporting affiliate and the number of affiliates surveyed. In the 1987 survey, all foreign affiliates having assets, sales, or net income in excess of $20 million were requested to submit full balance sheets and income statements, as well as all of the following information: reconciliation of retained earnings; sales data by industry; sales data by goods versus services; employee compensation information; the number of employees in each industry in which the affiliate had sales; the number of employees whose compensation was subject to collective bargaining; the composition of external debt by where carried on the balance sheet; depreciation and depletion charges; plant and equipment expenditures by type of expenditure; interest receipts and payments; taxes; research and development expenditures; US merchandise exports and imports by product, country of destination or origin, and (for imports) intended use; and detail by state for total employment and manufacturing employment, acres of land owned, acres of mineral rights owned or leased, and the gross book value of land, plant, and equipment by use.

These affiliates also had to report the name (unless the owner was an individual), country, and industry of the first foreign parent and the ultimate beneficial owner, the affiliate's ownership structure, and the existence of any foreign-government ownership of 5 percent or more. Detailed information on transactions and positions between the affiliate and its foreign parent and other members of the foreign parent group were also required. Affiliates not meeting the $20 million criterion but whose assets, sales, or net income were above $1 million had to report a smaller amount of information, and affiliates not meeting the $1 million criterion were required to provide data on assets, sales, and income only.

The results of each benchmark survey are contained in a volume published by the BEA. Highlights of the surveys appear in the *Survey of Current Business*.

The sample surveys include quarterly surveys of balance of payments data. The sample is selected to cover about 90 percent of the universe in value terms. Items from these surveys that are also part of the balance of payments accounts appear in the March, June, September, and December issues of the *Survey of Current Business*. An estimate of the international direct investment position of the United States appears in the June issue, and more detailed estimates of this position as well as balance of payments items appear in the August issue. Selected financial and operating data are surveyed annually; sample coverage is 92 to 93 percent in value terms. Highlights of this survey are also reported in the *Survey of Current Business*, and more detailed information is published in a separate volume.

All US businesses newly acquired or established by foreign owners must be reported to the BEA within 45 days of the transaction; this reporting must include a limited amount of financial and operating data as well as information on the foreign parent, the ultimate beneficial owner, and the cost of the acquisition or establishment. Information from these filings is summarized annually in the *Survey of Current Business*.

Adequacy of the BEA Data

Critics of the BEA have alleged that the agency misses a significant share of FDI; that inconsistencies in the data cast doubt on the validity of the numbers; that not enough information is collected; that there is systematic mismeasurement of the industrial composition of foreign holdings; and that the limits on reporting imposed by the commitment to confidentiality are excessive. We consider each of these criticisms in turn.

Noncompliance

The question of whether substantial foreign holdings of US assets go unreported to the BEA is addressed in Chapter 1. Interviews with BEA personnel convinced us that the BEA does an adequate job of monitoring compliance with the filing requirement of firms meeting the 10 percent ownership criterion. Within the Commerce Department, for example, the International Trade Administration compiles a list of all foreign acquisitions of US enterprises reported in the press; the BEA uses this list to cross-check its filings and follows up wherever it appears that an enterprise that should have filed has not done so. As with many other types of government reporting (e.g., the filing of income tax returns), the accuracy of the information filed with the BEA depends largely on voluntary compliance. That is, although accurate filing is mandatory, the forms are generally not audited unless discrepancies are observed or errors suspected. All forms are reviewed for internal consistency and completeness, and reviews are conducted to ensure consistency across reports and with related data filed elsewhere with the government.

Under such a system of "mandatory voluntary" compliance there is always some room for abuse. However, there is little incentive to falsify data on FDI submitted to the BEA, since the information is confidential and cannot be used for investigative or regulatory purposes. We therefore have no reason to believe that any significant degree of misreporting takes place. At any rate, the alternative to mandatory voluntary reporting would be a policing system that could prove oppressive as well as costly.

Inconsistencies

Critics have noted several apparent discrepancies that appear to indicate flaws in the BEA data. Discrepancies have been alleged to occur within the US data themselves, and data gathered by certain foreign governments relating to their residents' direct investment in the United States have been found not to reconcile with the corresponding US data. For example, Canadian data on Canadian direct investment in the United States show more such investment than do the US data.

We have been able to find no discrepancies within the US data. One reason such discrepancies are perceived is that, as we have noted, analysts often misinterpret the data. Part of the blame for the confusion does, however, rest with the BEA. The distinctions between different data series might not be clear to many users of the data, and no layperson's guide to the data exists. Descriptions of methodologies are provided in the benchmark publications and in articles in the *Survey of Current Business*, which has also published articles explaining the differences in the data series. However, these explanations are often quite technical and make for difficult reading for persons not trained in balance of payments or financial accounting. Our understanding is that the BEA is now preparing a written guide to the FDI data aimed at persons with nontechnical backgrounds. We have also found that BEA personnel were quite willing and able to provide us with satisfactory explanations of the data when asked.

The observed cross-national discrepancies partly result from differences in definitions and standards applied. For example, Canada classifies as outward direct investment some holdings that the United States classifies as inward portfolio investment. The BEA reports that it has cross-checked its data on inward FDI from Canada with the data collected by the government of Canada, and, after adjusting for differences in definitions and standards, found the two series to be over 95 percent reconcilable.

It would be desirable for all governments to work toward harmonizing their definitions and standards concerning FDI and how it is reported. This would facilitate international comparisons and thus make the task of the researcher much easier. Such a harmonization could be undertaken within the context of the Committee on Investment and Multinational Enterprise of the Organization for Economic Cooperation and Development (OECD), or perhaps through the United Nations Center on Transnational Corporations. Until then, differences in definitions and standards will remain a fact of life with which analysts must live.

Insufficient Information

There are evident limitations on the range of questions that can be answered using BEA data. For example, there is no way to use the present data to produce an exact accounting of the sources of growth in the assets of foreign firms. Such data would be useful, but we are assured by the BEA that it would be close to impossible to collect them. However, the fact that there are useful data not being collected by the BEA does not imply that the BEA data that exist are useless. In fact, as we have shown, the data can be used to get a quite good picture of trends in the US direct investment position. By international standards the US data are actually quite good: a recent report by the British Royal Institute for International Affairs indicates that US data on FDI are more detailed than those published by any of the other Group of Five nations.

One possible approach to improving data collection would be to convene a group of researchers who have used the BEA data, along with BEA personnel themselves, to identify the holes that do exist. The BEA has already convened such a group to examine the information collected on outward FDI. A similar group for inward FDI would be desirable.

Expansion of the BEA's data collection would require augmenting the BEA's limited resources. In addition, under the Paperwork Reduction Act, the Office of Management and Budget would have to permit the expansion. Reporting companies would also have to devote additional resources to fulfilling the reporting requirements, and this could adversely affect their willingness to comply. The question that must be asked is whether the marginal value of any additional information is greater than the marginal cost of generating it.

Misclassifications

In the BEA's published data series, all investment by any one enterprise is classified by the principal industry of that enterprise. This can cause obvious problems when the activities of the enterprise are in fact diversified across industries. Thus, for example, the US manufacturing operations of certain Japanese automotive firms are classified under the major industry of their US affiliates and therefore are listed under wholesale trade rather than manufacturing.

One answer to this problem would be to augment the data on consolidated enterprises with data collected at the "establishment" level—that is, data that pertain to individual facilities within a consolidated enterprise, such as manufacturing plants. Such a compilation is technically possible using raw data already being collected by the Census Bureau. As we have noted, the most recent benchmark survey of inward FDI was postponed for two years precisely to allow cross-referencing of Census and BEA data. Some cross-referencing has already been accomplished on a pilot basis, and efforts are under way to extend this compilation.

Another approach would be for the BEA itself to collect data at the establishment level. In fact, beginning with the 1987 benchmark survey the BEA will have data on sales and employment by industry of sales. These data will approximate data collected at the enterprise level, although the correlation will not be perfect.

There are some legal, budgetary, and possibly bureaucratic problems associated with the effort to link BEA and Census data. We believe, nonetheless, that much potentially important policy analysis depends upon such an effort. For example, comparisons of the relative performance of foreign-controlled and domestically controlled operations in particular industries can be meaningfully accomplished only when this linking is complete. Only then will it be possible to answer such questions as whether US affiliates of Japanese automobile firms achieve higher labor productivities than do domestically controlled operations, and whether foreign-controlled semiconductor manufacturing facilities are mere "screwdriver" (i.e., assembly only) operations compared to US—controlled ones. We therefore recommend that the US government attach a high level of priority to this linkage effort, and that legislation be introduced if needed to break down any legal barriers that might impede its progress. Elements of a bill introduced in Congress by Senator Frank H. Murkowski (R-AK) are designed to do just that.

We also believe that the type of policy analysis we have described will require that industry-specific data be more finely disaggregated than they are at present. In some cases, publication of the disaggregated data might conflict with company-specific confidentiality requirements. We address this matter in the next section.

Limitations Due to Confidentiality

Because of the requirement of confidentiality, company-level data collected by the BEA are not generally available to persons outside the agency either for research or for policy formulation (although consultants to the BEA and contractors performing research for the BEA can have access under some circumstances). This restriction is not arbitrary; confidentiality serves to ensure that the information submitted to the BEA is accurate, because there is little incentive for a reporting enterprise to submit false or inaccurate data. Most policy analysis and formulation does not require that researchers or policymakers have access to specific company-level data.

Nonetheless, we believe that the extent of confidentiality presently observed in BEA data gathering is in some respects overdone. We would see no harm, for example, in allowing the reporting firms themselves to decide whether their submissions will be open to the public. In Japan, information on inward direct investment by individual companies is open for public scrutiny unless the company requests that it not be; if the company does so request, its wishes are observed scrupulously. It is also easy to envisage a multitiered approach to confidentiality, wherein certain types of company-specific information would be open to the public while more sensitive information would remain closed. These two ideas could be combined: companies could elect which tiers would be open and which closed. Such an arrangement would surely not have a chilling effect on FDI. One could also envisage establishing a time limit on confidentiality, whereby after some specified period company records would become open to the public.

Critics of the BEA note that its records on FDI cannot be scrutinized by high government officials for investigative purposes even in times of national emergency, even though other files normally kept confidential (Internal Revenue Service 1040 forms, for example) can be released to certain officials for emergency national security purposes. There has been no known abuse of these provisions to date. Arguably, the BEA records should also be subject to some sort of national-emergency provision. Such a provision, were it deemed desirable, would require a legislative change.

We have already indicated that linkage of BEA and Census data could make possible some useful policy analysis that cannot now be accomplished. One requirement for meaningful intraindustry comparisons of foreign- and domestically controlled operations will be access to data at a disaggregated level. There is no reason, however, why the researchers must have access to company-specific information. BEA and Census personnel could combine company-specific records into aggregated data files that do not divulge confidential information, and these files could then be provided to the researcher.

This sort of service is already provided by the BEA and the Census Bureau on a limited basis. The researcher must reimburse the agencies for the cost of the data preparation. Some users of this data report that it is difficult and costly to gain access to this type of service. The Census Bureau in particular has been cited as difficult to work with, and there is some feeling that the price charged to users for "customized" data from the Census Bureau is excessive. Since research based on census information is in at least some respects a public good, pricing the service above its marginal cost could be misguided policy. This issue notwithstanding, fruitful research using both BEA and Census data has been accomplished. The present study is an example of research done largely on the basis of data readily available from the BEA and other government sources.

Appendix B   Industrial-Organization Explanations of Foreign Direct Investment

In this appendix we survey briefly some of the main arguments that fall within the general category of industrial-organization explanations of foreign direct investment. Some of these arguments are based on the classical theory of industrial organization, whereas others are based on newer, game-theoretic approaches. The interested reader is referred to the sources listed in the bibliography for more complete reviews of this literature. Perhaps the most detailed review is provided in Caves (1982), although this reference does not cover some important work done in recent years. A more recent article by Rugman (1986) bridges some of this gap.

Generally, industrial-organization theories of FDI can be divided into two categories: those that focus on the internal characteristics of multinational firms, and those that focus on rivalry among such firms. A number of theories rely on arguments from both categories, and hence the two categories are not wholly disjoint. Nonetheless, they do provide some basis for a taxonomical treatment of the subject.

Internal Characteristics

The work most often cited as seminal in creating this basis is the 1959 doctoral dissertation of Stephen Hymer, published posthumously in 1976. Hymer first articulated the now widely accepted notion that a firm whose operations cross national boundaries faces costs that a firm whose operations are limited to one nation does not. These extra costs include those of managing geographically widespread operations and those of dealing with different languages, cultures, technical standards, and customer preferences. Hymer argued that for a firm to overcome the handicaps posed by these extra costs, it must possess internal, firm-specific advantages over its rivals. He speculated that these advantages largely took the form of economies of scale or of superior product technology.

A second very influential early work was that by John Dunning (1958). This work was largely empirical in nature. Dunning examined manufacturing operations in the United Kingdom controlled by US–based firms. He found that these operations generally paid higher wages and were characterized by higher rates of labor productivity and new product innovation than their UK–controlled rivals. Dunning's work, although done quite independently of Hymer's, seemed to confirm many of Hymer's speculations.

145

Much of the work since Hymer and Dunning has attempted to pin down the firm-specific advantages that drive FDI. Aharoni (1966) noted the importance of imperfect information about markets as a determinant of FDI flows; Vernon (1968, 1974) pointed out the linkage between the product life cycle in technology and the shift from exports to direct investment among US firms; Kindleberger (1969) noted the role of firm-specific advantages other than technology, such as organizational and marketing skills. Caves (1971) summarized these developments by noting that the advantages possessed by multinational enterprises can include any of a number of intangible assets, including organizational and marketing skills and product and process technologies.

Buckley and Casson (1976) suggested a still broader interpretation of the motivations for FDI that has since become more or less the standard point of departure. They observed that for the multinational enterprise to service non-home-nation markets via direct investment rather than alternative modes of doing business (e.g., exporting or licensing) there must exist some "internalization" advantage for the firm to do so. That is, there must be economies associated with a firm exploiting a market opportunity through internal operations rather than through arm's-length transactions such as the sale of rights to the firm's intangible assets to other firms. These economies might be associated with costs (including opportunity costs) of contract enforcement or of maintenance of quality or other standards. Buckley and Casson noted that, where these costs are absent, firms very often do use licensing or franchising as a means of serving international markets. For example, Coca-Cola franchises the right to market its products in many nations where contract enforcement is not a problem, but the firm directly controls operations in nations where enforcement is a problem.

Dunning (1988) has emphasized that the advantages of internalization must interact with both firm-specific and locational advantages to explain FDI.

The effort to define the advantages of internalization is ultimately part of the theory of why firms exist. This effort has generated a large literature, which is surveyed by Rugman (1986). A more recent development has been the attempt to embed theories of FDI in formal models of international trade; see, for example, Helpman and Krugman (1985).

Intraindustry Rivalry

The possibility that rivalry among firms operating in the same industry, but not necessarily in the same country or countries, can affect FDI behavior was suggested by Hymer both in his doctoral dissertation and in some later work (see, e.g., Hymer and Rowthorne 1970). To some extent rivalry drives FDI in

Raymond Vernon's work (e.g., 1968) as well. The same idea appears in an influential book by Seev Hirsch (1967).

Knickerbocker (1973) noted a "follow the leader" pattern in the timing of FDI by US firms. He interpreted this phenomenon as a rational response to oligopolistic rivalry. Other studies have detected similar patterns in the overseas activities of non–US firms (Flowers 1976). Also, detailed studies of certain industries have confirmed Knickerbocker's findings for US firms (e.g., Yu and Ito 1988). Finally, Graham (1978, 1989) suggests that intraindustry FDI may take place as an "exchange of threat," in which firms invade each others' home markets as part of an oligopolistic rivalry.

References

Aharoni, Yair. 1966. *The Foreign Investment Decision Process.* Boston: Harvard University Graduate School of Business Administration.

Anderson, Jack. 1989. "Is America For Sale?" *Parade* (16 April).

Bacow, Lawrence. 1987. "Understanding Foreign Investment in Real Estate." *Working Papers 12.* Cambridge: Massachusetts Institute of Technology Center for Real Estate Development.

———. 1988. "The Internationalization of the U.S. Real Estate Industry." *Working Papers 16.* Cambridge: Massachusetts Institute of Technology Center for Real Estate Development.

Becker, Michael. 1989. *Myths About Foreign Investment.* Washington: Citizens for a Sound Economy Foundation.

Bergsten, C. Fred. 1974. "Coming Investment Wars?" *Foreign Affairs* 53, no. 1 (October): 135–52.

Bergsten, C. Fred, Thomas Horst, and Theodore H. Moran. 1978. *American Multinationals and American Interests.* Washington: Brookings Institution.

Brander, James A., and Barbara J. Spencer. 1985. "Export Subsidies and Market Share Rivalry." *Journal of International Economics* 18, no. 1/2 (February): 83–100.

Brecher, Richard A., and Carlos F. Diaz-Alejandro. 1977. "Tariffs, Foreign Capital, and Immiserizing Growth." *Journal of International Economics* 7, no. 4 (November): 317–22.

Buckley, Peter J., and Mark C. Casson. 1976. *The Future of Multinational Enterprise.* London: Macmillan.

Burstein, Daniel. 1988. *Yen: Japan's New Financial Empire and Its Threat to America.* New York: Simon and Schuster.

Cantwell, John. 1989. *Technological Innovation and Multinational Corporations.* London: Blackwell.

Carter, Barry E. 1988. *International Economic Sanctions: Improving the Haphazard U.S. Legal Regime.* Cambridge: Cambridge University Press.

Caves, Richard E. 1971. "International Corporations: The Industrial Economics of Foreign Investment." *Economica* 38, no. 141: 1–27.

———. 1982. *Multinational Enterprise and Economic Analysis.* Cambridge: Cambridge University Press.

Cline, William R. 1989. *United States External Adjustment and the World Economy.* Washington: Institute for International Economics.

Dunning, John H. 1958. *American Investment in British Manufacturing Industry.* London: George Allen & Unwin.

———. 1988. "The Eclectic Paradigm of International Production: A Restatement and Some Possible Extensions." *Journal of International Business Studies* 19, no. 1: 1–31.

Flowers, Ed B. 1976. "Oligopolistic Reactions in European and Canadian Direct Investment in the United States." *Journal of International Business Studies* 7, no. 3: 43–55.

Forbes, Malcolm S. 1988. "Before Japan Buys Too Much of the U.S.A." *Forbes* (25 January): 17.

Frantz, Douglas, and Catherine Collins. 1989. *Selling Out: How We Are Letting Japan Buy Our Land, Our Industries, Our Financial Institutions, and Our Future.* Chicago: Contemporary Books.

Froot, Kenneth, and Jeremy Stein. 1989. "Exchange Rates and Foreign Direct Investment: An Imperfect Capital Markets Approach." *NBER Working Papers* 2914. Cambridge, MA: National Bureau of Economic Research.

Glickman, Norman, and Douglas Woodward. 1989. *The New Competitors: How Foreign Investors Are Changing the U.S. Economy.* New York: Basic Books.

Graham, Edward M. 1978. "Transatlantic Investment by Multinational Firms: A Rivalistic Phenomenon?" *Journal of Post Keynesian Economics* 1, no. 1 (Fall): 82–99.

———. 1989. "Strategic Interaction Among Multinational Firms and International Direct Investment." In C. N. Pitelis and R. Sugden, eds., *The Nature of the Transnational Firm.* London: Routledge, Chapman and Hall (forthcoming).

Haber, L. F. 1971. *The Chemical Industry, 1900-1930.* Oxford: Oxford University Press.

Hastings, Max. 1984. *Overlord and the Battle for Normandy.* New York: Simon and Schuster.

Helpman, Elhanan, and Paul R. Krugman. 1985. *Market Structure and Foreign Trade.* Cambridge, MA: MIT Press.

———. 1989. *Trade Policy and Market Structure.* Cambridge: MIT Press.

Hirsch, Seev. 1967. *Location of Industry and International Competitiveness.* Oxford: Oxford University Press.

Hooper, Peter, and Catherine L. Mann. 1987. "The U.S. External Deficit: Its Causes and Persistence." *International Finance Discussion Papers* 316. Washington: Federal Reserve Board.

Hufbauer, G. C., and F. M. Adler. 1968. "Overseas Manufacturing Investment and the Balance of Payments." *Tax Policy Research Studies* 1 (US Department of the Treasury). Washington: Government Printing Office.

Hufbauer, Gary Clyde, and Jeffrey J. Schott. 1983. *Economic Sanctions in Support of Foreign Policy Goals.* POLICY ANALYSES IN INTERNATIONAL ECONOMICS 6. Washington: Institute for International Economics (October).

Hull, Cordell. 1948. *Memoirs* (2 vols.). New York: Macmillan.

Hymer, Stephen H. 1976. *The International Operations of National Firms.* Cambridge: MIT Press (originally, Ph.D. diss., Massachusetts Institute of Technology, accepted 1959).

Hymer, Stephen H., and Robert Rowthorne. 1970. "Multinational Firms and International Oligopoly: The Non-American Challenge." In Charles P. Kindleberger, ed., *The International Corporation: A Symposium.* Cambridge: MIT Press, 57–91.

Jackson, John H. 1977. *Legal Problems of International Economic Relations.* St. Paul, MN: West.

Jackson, James K. 1987. *Japan: Increasing Investment in the United States* (report #87–747E). Washington: Congressional Research Service.

Jahnke, Art. 1989. "Six Flags Over Boston." *Boston* (May).

Julius, DeAnne, and Stephen Thomsen. 1988. "Foreign-owned Firms, Trade, and Economic Integration." In *Tokyo Club Papers* 2. London: Royal Institute of International Affairs.

Kindleberger, Charles P. 1969. *American Business Abroad: Six Lectures on Foreign Direct Investment.* New Haven: Yale University Press.

Knickerbocker, Frederick T. 1973. *Oligopolistic Reaction and Multinational Enterprise.* Boston: Harvard University Graduate School of Business Administration.

Lewis, Jordan D. 1982. "Technology, Enterprise, and American Economic Growth." *Science* 215:1204–11.

Magaziner, Ira C., and Robert B. Reich. 1982. *Minding America's Business: The Decline and Rise of the American Economy.* New York: Vintage Books.

Ministry of International Trade and Industry. *Third Basic Survey on Japanese Business Activities Abroad.* Tokyo: Ministry of International Trade and Industry (forthcoming).

Moran, Theodore H. 1989. "The Globalization of America's Defense Industries: What Is the Threat? How Can It Be Managed?" Washington: Georgetown University School of Foreign Service (mimeographed).

Moran, Theodore H., and Charles S. Pearson. 1988. "Tread Carefully in the Field of TRIP Measures." *The World Economy* 11, no. 1 (March): 119–34.

Morgan Guaranty Trust Company. 1989. "Foreign Direct Investment in the United States." *World Financial Markets* no. 2 (29 June): 1–11.

Mundell, Robert. 1987. "A New Deal on Exchange Rates." Presented at the Japan–United States Symposium on Exchange Rates and Macroeconomics, Tokyo (29–30 January).

Nomura Research Institute. 1989. *Nomura Medium-Term Outlook for Japan and the World.* Tokyo: Nomura Research Institute.

Organization for Economic Cooperation and Development. 1987. *Controls and Impediments Affecting Inward Direct Investment in OECD Member Countries.* Paris: OECD.

Peterson, Peter G. 1989. "Japanese Mergers and Acquisitions in the United States: The Deals and the Dealmakers." Presented at a conference by the same name sponsored by the Japan Society, New York (13 July).

Prestowitz, Clyde. 1988. *Trading Places: How We Allowed the Japanese to Take the Lead.* New York: Basic Books.

Rohatyn, Felix. 1989. "America's Economic Dependence." *Foreign Affairs* 68, no. 1: 53–65.

Rugman, Alan M. 1986. "New Theories of Multinational Enterprises: An Assessment of Internalisation Theory." *Bulletin of Economic Research* 38, no. 2 (May): 101–18.

Scholes, Myron, and Mark Wolfson. 1988. "The Effects of Changes in Tax Laws on Corporate Reorganization Activity." Stanford, CA: Stanford University (mimeographed).

Shapiro, Carl, and Joseph E. Stiglitz. 1984. "Equilibrium Unemployment as a Worker Discipline Device." *American Economic Review* 74, no. 3 (June 1984): 433–44.

Slemrod, Joel. 1989. "Tax Effects on Foreign Direct Investment in the U.S: Evidence from a Cross-Country Comparison." Presented at the National Bureau of Economic Research Conference on International Aspects of Taxation, Cambridge, MA (February).

Spencer, Linda M. 1988. *American Assets: An Examination of Foreign Investment in the United States.* Arlington, VA: Congressional Economic Leadership Institute.

Terrell, Henry S., Robert S. Dohner, and Barbara Lowrey. 1989. "The U.S. and U.K. Activities of Japanese Banks." *International Finance Discussion Papers* 316. Washington: Federal Reserve (September).

Tolchin, Martin, and Susan Tolchin. 1988. *Buying Into America: How Foreign Money Is Changing the Face of Our Nation.* New York: Times Books.

Ulan, Michael, and William G. Dewald. 1989. "The U.S. Net International Investment Position: Misstated and Misunderstood." In James A. Dorn and William A. Niskanen, eds., *Dollars, Deficit, and Trade.* Boston: Kluwer Academic Publishers.

US Congress. House. Committee on Strategic and Military Affairs. 1939. *Strategic and Critical Raw Materials,* hearings, 76th Cong., 1st sess.

_____. Joint Economic Committee. 1981. *International Competition in Advanced Industrial Sectors: Trade and Development in the Semiconductor Industry.* Report prepared by Michael Borrus, James Millstein, and John Zysman, 97th Cong., 2nd sess.

_____. Senate. Committee on Military Affairs. 1944. *Economic and Political Aspects of International Cartels.* Report prepared by Corwin Edwards, *Subcommittee on War Mobilization Monograph* 1, 78th Cong., 2nd sess.

_____. Senate. Special Committee Investigating Petroleum Resources. 1946. *American Petroleum Interests in Foreign Countries,* hearings, 79th Cong., 1st sess.

US Department of the Treasury. 1988. "Survey of G-7 Laws and Regulations on Foreign Direct Investment." Washington: US Department of the Treasury (internal memorandum available on request from the Office of Foreign Investment).

US General Accounting Office. 1988. *Foreign Investment: Growing Japanese Presence in U.S. Auto Industry* (GAO/NSIAD-88-111, March). Washington: Government Printing Office.

Vernon, Raymond. 1966. "International Investment and International Trade in the Product Cycle." *Quarterly Journal of Economics* 83, no. 1 (February): 190–207.

_____. 1971. "Multinational Enterprise and National Security." *Adelphi Papers* 74. London: Institute for Strategic Studies.

_____. 1974. "The Location of Economic Activity." In John H. Dunning, ed., *Economic Analysis and the Multinational Enterprise.* London: George Allen & Unwin.

Wilkins, Mira. 1970. *The Emergence of Multinational Enterprise: American Business Abroad from the Colonial Era to 1914.* Cambridge: Harvard University Press.

_____. 1974. *The Maturing of Multinational Enterprise: American Business Abroad from 1914 to 1970.* Cambridge: Harvard University Press.

_____. 1989. *The History of Foreign Investment in the United States.* Cambridge: Harvard University Press.

Wilkins, Mira, and Frank Earnest Hill. 1964. *American Business Abroad: Ford on Six Continents.* Detroit: Wayne State University Press.

Yu, Chwo-Ming J., and Kiyohiko Ito. 1988. "Oligopolistic Reaction and Foreign Direct Investment: The Case of the U.S. Tire and Textile Industries." *Journal of International Business Studies* 19, no. 3: 449–60.

Zilg, Gerard C. 1974. *DuPont: Behind the Nylon Curtain.* Englewood Cliffs, NJ: Prentice-Hall.

Index

Regulation of foreign investment;
Taxation
alternatives to, 10–16, 146
definition of, 7–10, 37
in Group of Five countries, 24–26
mechanics of, 16–18, 36–37
Foreign direct investment by the United
States. *See* Outward Foreign direct
investment
Foreign direct investment in the United
States. *See also* "Fire sale" issue;
International rules for foreign
investment; Japanese investment in
the United States; National security;
US policy toward foreign investment
by US allies, 85–91
benefits of, 3–4, 146
causes of, 2–3, 28–30, 145–47. *See
also* Dollar, US; Current account,
US; Debtor status of United States
characteristics of, 54–62
compared to other industrial
countries, 2, 5, 24–26, 107–09
cost of capital explanation, 2–3,
28–30
effect on US economy, 3–4, 13,
45–64, 111–12. *See also*
Employment; Foreign affiliates in
the United States; Value added
extent of, 1, 7–26, 138
growth of, 1–2, 11–13, 15, 18, 25–26
industrial organization explanation,
2–3, 28–37, 45–46, 145–47
Japanese share of, 19–21. *See also*
Japan
measurement of, 1, 9–16, 51. *See also*
Bureau of Economic Analysis; FDI
stock ratio
prospects for, 43–44, 125–29
sources of, 2, 19, 27–44. *See also
particular countries*
value of, 35, 44, 50–51
Foreign trade. *See* Trade, international
France
foreign investment in, 25–26, 107
Ford subsidiaries in during World
War II, 77
relations with the United States
during Vietnam War, 74–75

General Agreement on Tariffs and Trade
(GATT), 102–04, 118–19, 129, 131.
See also International rules on foreign
investment
Uruguay Round, 102, 103, 118

General Dynamics, 87
General Electric, 40–41
General Motors, nationality of, 8
Germany. *See also* Ford Motor
Company; Standard Oil, SOCONY
access of US to German technology
after World War II, 79–80
foreign investment in, 25–26
relationship with foreign-owned firms
during World War II, 76–80
US affiliate bank assets, 22
Glass-Steagall Act, 118
Great Britain, 145
corporate taxation in, 38–39
Department of Trade and Industry,
108–09
foreign direct investment in, 25, 87,
108–09
investment in United States by, 3, 8,
33–34, 45–46
manufacturing operations of US-
based firms in, 145
Monopolies and Mergers
Commission, 108–09, 123
policy toward foreign investment, 108
subsidiaries of US companies in,
during World War II, 78, 125
US affiliate bank assets, 22
Greece, US affiliate bank assets, 22
"Greenfield" production facilities, 16,
50, 98. *See also* Subsidiaries of foreign
firms in the United States
Gross National Product (GNP), US
foreign share of, 11, 13, 15, 30–33
manufacturing share in, 36
ratio of foreign direct investment
stock to, 30
Group of Five countries (G-5), 114. *See
also particular countries*
foreign direct investment in, 24–26
Group of Seven countries (G-7), 116,
126. *See also particular countries*
policy coordination by, 126

Hayes, Walter, 76–77
Headquarters effect, 47, 52–53, 92. 55,
62, *See also* Foreign affiliates in the
United States; Research and
development
High technology. *See also* Military
technology
decline of US market share in, 88–91
importance to national security,
83–86

Home-nation rights and responsibilities, proposed, 126–27. *See also* International rules on foreign investment

Honda, 41, 61
competition for US manufacturing site, 105
nationality of, 8
opening of plant in Marysville, Ohio, 17

Hong Kong, US affiliate bank assets, 22

Huls AG, 99, 120

Hymer, Stephen, 145

IEEPA. *See* International Emergency Economic Powers Act

Import quotas. *See* Protectionism

Imports by foreign affiliates, 3–4, 46, 49–51, 55–58, 60–61, 64, 112, 130
cost to United States, 3–4

Incentives for investment. *See* Investment

Income distribution, 66

Income repatriation, 38, 65

Income taxes. *See* Taxation

Indonesia, US affiliate bank assets, 22

Industrial-organization explanations for foreign direct investment, 2–3, 28–37, 145–47. *See also* foreign direct investment in the United States

Industrial policy, 53–54, 87, 116, 119. *See also* Investment

Inflation, 48. *See also* Employment; Nonaccelerating Inflation Rate of Unemployment (NAIRU)

Insurance industry, US
compensation of employees in, 57
foreign control of, 33

Integration. *See* Vertical integration

Interest rates, Federal Reserve Bank control of, 48–49

International accord on foreign investment, proposed, 81, 125–29

International banking. *See* Banking, international

International capital flows. *See* Capital flows, international

Interstate banking. *See* Banking sector, US

International Emergency Economic Powers Act (IEEPA), 82, 84, 97, 124–25

International rules on foreign investment, 71–72. *See also* General Agreement on Tariffs and Trade

(GATT); National treatment; Reciprocity; US policy toward foreign investment
negotiation of new accord, proposed, 125–29

Investment. *See also* Foreign direct investment; Portfolio investment
incentives for, 53–54, 69, 105–06, 118, 128

Investment companies, as form of direct investment, 20–21

Investment wars, 130–31

Inward foreign direct investment. *See* Foreign direct investment in the United States

Ireland, US affiliate bank assets, 22

Israel, US affiliate bank assets, 22

Italy, US affiliate bank assets, 22

Japan, 85. *See also* Automobile industry, US; Banking sector, US; Electronics industry, US; Foreign affiliates in the United States; Foreign direct investment in the United States; Yen-dollar exchange rate
acquisitions in United States, 3, 16–21, 34, 54–55, 126, 130
color television production by, 40–41, 62
as exporter of capital, 33
foreign direct investment in, 25
Keiretsu (business associations), 60
Ministry of International Trade and Industry (MITI), 91, 127
relationship with foreign-owned firms during World War II, 77–78
role in US automobile industry, 17, 41–42, 50–51, 56, 61–62, 70, 141
role in US banking, 19, 21, 22, 42–43, 70–71
role in US manufacturing, 19
stock market, 35, 37
US policy toward investment by, 119–20
withholding of technology from United States, 119–20

Japanese firms in the United States, 9, 54–55. *See also* Foreign affiliates in the United States
characteristics of, 17–18, 59–62, 92, 118, 120, 130
employment by, 19
import propensity of, 46, 50–51, 55–61, 64, 112, 130

performance requirements toward, 119–20

value added of, 18–19

Japanese policy toward foreign direct investment, 25, 53–54, 107–08, 126–27

corporate taxation policy, 38–39

Joint ventures, 98.

Keiretsu. See Japan

Korea, Republic of, US affiliate bank assets, 22

Kyocera, particpation in US Tomahawk missile program, 91

Labor, bargaining power of, 47

Lobbying in United States by foreign firms, 65, 68–69

Local content requirements, 123

Lockheed, 87

Legislation, US, 7, 141. *See also* Bryant amendment, Exon-Florio amendment, Omnibus Trade and Competitiveness Act of 1988, US policy toward foreign investment

Licensing, compulsory, 124

Limited partnerships, underreporting of foreign investment in, 9, 23

Luxembourg, US affiliate bank assets, 22

Managerial expertise, as reason for foreign investment, 27–30, 34, 47, 145–46

Manufacturing, US. *See also* Employment; Foreign affiliates in the United States; *particular industries*

compensation of employees in, 57–58

employment in, 13, 14, 24

foreign share of, 2, 9, 13, 17, 20, 33, 141

share of US gross national product, 36

Marcos, Ferdinand, 23

Market value

of foreign assets in the United States, 11, 12

of US assets overseas, 12

Matra, 100

Matsuhita, acquisition of Motorola, 41

Mazda, US assembly plant, 69

Measurement of foreign direct investment. *See* Foreign direct investment in the United States

Mergers and Acquisitions by foreign firms, 17–18, 36–37, 98. *See also* Acquisition of US assets by foreign firms; Japan

screening of, 115, 121

Mexico, US affiliate bank assets, 22

Military technology. *See also* Compulsory licensing; Defense Department, US; National security

access to during wartime, 75, 79–81

performance requirements for, 80, 123–24

US control of, 80–81, 85–88, 91–93, 122

Mining, US

compensation of employees in, 57

foreign share of, 33

regulation of, 96, 105

Ministry of International Trade and Industry (MITI). *See* Japan

Mobil, 7–8, 77

Monopolization. *See also* Sherman Antitrust Act

antitrust laws, 92–93

of US defense industry, 122–23

Monopolies and Mergers Commission. *See* United Kingdom

Monsanto, 99, 120

Motorola, 40–41

acquisition by Matsuhita, 41

Murkowski, Frank H., 141

NAIRU. *See* Nonaccelerating inflation rate of unemployment

National Association of Realtors, 23–24

National security, 73–93, 111, 115–17, 121–24. *See also* Defense Department, US; Military technology; US policy toward foreign investment

effect of foreign direct investment on, 4–5, 47, 53–54, 66–68, 73–93, 99, 121–25

John Walker spy case, 85

wartime investment by US allies and, 74, 85–91

National treatment standard, 53–54, 72, 96, 109, 112, 127

Nationality of multinational firms, 7–8

NATO (North Atlantic Treaty Organization), 74. *See also particular countries*

Netherlands, The. *See also* Royal Dutch-Shell

corporate taxation in, 38–39

investment in United States by, 8, 22, 34

Neutrality. *See* National treatment standard. *See also* Establishment; Reciprocity

Nonaccelerating inflation rate of unemployment (NAIRU), 48–49. *See also* Employment; Inflation

Nonlisted firms. *See* Privately held firms

Northrop, 87

Norway, US affiliate bank assets, 22

OECD. *See* Organization for Economic Cooperation and Development

Office of Management and Budget, US (OMB)
representative on Committee on Foreign Investment in the United States (CFIUS), 98

Office of the US Trade Representative. *See* US Trade Representative, Office of

Omnibus Trade and Competitveness Act of 1988, 95, 97, 113–14. *See also* Bryant amendment; Exon-Florio amendment

Organization for Economic Cooperation and Development (OECD), 106–7, 128–29, 140
Committee on International Investment and Multinational Enterprise (CIIME) of, 106–07, 140
Declaration on International Investment and Multinational Enterprise of 1978, 102

Organization of Petroleum Exporting Countries (OPEC), 135

Outward foreign direct investment, US, 2, 101–04, 140

Ownership of US assets, foreign. *See* Foreign direct investment in the United States

Payments, balance of. *See* Balance of payments, US

Performance requirements, 112, 118–20. *See also* National security; US policy toward foreign investment
international rules on, 125–29
at state level, 119
during wartime, 80–81, 85–91

Petroleum industry, US, foreign share in, 33

Philips, nationality of, 8

Plants, manufacturing, 16–17, 50. *See also* Subsidiaries of foreign firms in the United States

Political effects of foreign direct investment, 4, 65–72
political influence of foreign firms, 68–69

Portfolio investment, 9, 28, 29, 32, 45, 139. *See also* Financial markets
in real estate, 23–24
and tax policy, 38–39

Profitability, effect of foreign ownership on, 27–28

Protectionism, 39–40, 65–68, 126. *See also* Voluntary export restraints
cost to consumers, 70–71
and investment in manufacturing, 39–40
quotas, 70
tariffs, 66–68

Privately held firms, reporting by, 114

Public reaction to foreign investment, US, 1, 18, 59

Quotas. *See* Protectionism

R&D. *See* Research and development

Real estate, US
extent of foreign holdings, 9, 21–26
Japanese holdings in, 23–24, 26

Reciprocity of treatment of foreign and domestic firms, 96, 112, 117–18, 121. *See also* US policy toward foreign investment

Regulation of foreign investment. *See also* International rules on foreign investment; US policy toward foreign direct investment
by the United States, 4–5, 85–89, 97–100

Reporting requirements, 97–100. *See also* International rules on foreign investment; US policy toward foreign investment
of Bureau of Economic Analysis, 23, 100–01, 113–14, 135–43
of Securities and Exchange Commission, 101, 114

Research and development. *See also* Foreign affiliates in the United States; Headquarters effect
by foreign firms in the United States, 46, 52–53, 55, 58–59, 64, 80–81
by Japanese firms, 60–61, 120
foreign versus domestic firms, 58–59, 64
in wartime, 80–81

Retail industry, US

compensation of employees in, 57
foreign share in, 33
Rivalry, intraindustry, 146–47
Royal Dutch-Shell, 77
nationality of, 7–8

Savings, 29–30
Screening of foreign direct investment. *See also* International regulation of foreign investment; US policy toward foreign investment
in Canada, 107
in United States, 112, 115–17, 121
Seagram
acquisition of Tropicana, 17
nationality of, 8, 10
Secretary of the Treasury, US. *See* Treasury Department, US
Securities and Exchange Commission, US (SEC)
regulation of foreign investment, 101, 114
Security, national. *See* National security
Sematech, 121
Semiconductors, 89, 99–100
Shell. *See* Royal Dutch-Shell
Sherman Antitrust Act, 122
Siberian pipeline dispute, 104
SKF, nationality of, 8
SOCONY Vacuum Oil Company (now Mobil), joint venture with Standard Oil, 77–78
Soviet Union, 121
Spain, US affiliate bank assets, 22
Special security arrangement (SSA), 90
Standard Oil of New Jersey (now Exxon), joint venture with SOCONY Vacuum Oil Company, 77–78
Stanvac, 77
State and local policy toward foreign investment, 105–07. *See also* Investment
performance requirements, 119
State Department, US, 77–78
representation on Committee on Foreign Investment in the United States (CFIUS), 98
Stock of foreign direct investment, 12, 14, 20, 30–32. *See also* FDI stock ratio; Foreign direct investment in the United States
Stock market, Japanese. *See* Japan
Stock market, US. *See also* Financial markets crash of October 1987, 3, 48

role in foreign direct investment, 35, 37, 44, 114
"Strategic Investment Policy." *See* Industrial policy
Subsidiaries
of foreign firms in the United States, 16–19, 50
US subsidiaries in France during Vietnam War, 74–75
versus acquisition of US firms, 17, 19
Sugar industry, US, 39–40
Survey of Current Business, 135, 137–39
Sweden, investment in United States by, 8
Switzerland, US affiliate bank assets, 22

Taiwan (Republic of China), US affiliate bank assets, 22
Tariffs. *See* Protectionism
Taxation, 128. *See also* Investment
corporate, Canadian, 38–39
corporate, Japan, 38–39
corporate, United Kingdom, 38–39
corporate, US, 38–39, 44
effect on foreign investment, 37–39, 44, 69
Technology, 35. *See also* High technology; Military technology; National security
diffusion of through trade, 46–47, 52–53
withholding of by foreign suppliers, 92
Telecommunications, federal regulation of, 96
Televisions, color, production in the United States, 40–41, 62. *See also* Japan
Texaco, 77
Thomson, 40–41
Toshiba, 92
Toyota, competition for US plant, 69
Trade act. *See* Omnibus Trade and Competitiveness Act of 1988
Trade balance, US. *See also* Current account, US; Debtor status of the United States
effect of foreign investment on, 33–34, 44, 49–51, 56–58
exchange rate and, 50
Trade, international
benefits of, 45–47
in technology, 46–47, 52–53
by US firms versus foreign firms, 55–58

Trade policy, US. *See also* US Trade
Representative, Office of; United
States government
and national security, 53–54, 70–72
toward automobiles, 70
Trade-related investment measures
(TRIMs), 103–04, 119, 128
Trade Representative, US. *See* US Trade
Representative, Office of
Tradeable goods, 36. *See also*
Manufacturing, US
Trading with the Enemy Act (TWEA),
79, 81–82
Treasury Department, US
Secretary of the Treasury
as head of Committee on Foreign
Investment in the United States, 98
Treaty of Versailles, 79
TRIMs. *See* Trade-related investment
measures

Unemployment, US. *See also*
Employment, US; Foreign affiliates in
the United States
effect of foreign ownership on
nonaccelerating inflation rate of
(NAIRU), 48–49
Unitary taxation, 106. *See also* Taxation
United Kingdom. *See* Great Britain
United States government. *See*
Commerce Department; Congress,
US; Council on Economic Advisers;
Justice Department; Office of
Management and Budget; State
Department; Treasury Department;
US Trade Representative; US policy
toward foreign direct investment
US-Canada Free Trade Agreement, 102,
126–28
US Congress. *See* Congress, US
US policy toward foreign direct
investment, 95–109, 111–31. *See also*
Regulation of foreign investment

compared with other nations,
107–09, 123–28
corporate taxation, 38–39, 44
International Investment and Trade in
Services Survey act, 135, 136
neutrality, 95–96. *See also* National
treatment; Reciprocity
outward foreign investment, 101–04
US Trade Representative, Office of
representation on Committee on
Foreign Investment in the United
States (CFIUS), 98

Value added. *See also* Foreign affiliates
in the United States
by foreign firms, 11, 13, 15–16, 20,
57–58, 120
by Japanese firms, 61, 64, 120
Venezuela, US affiliate bank assets, 22
Vertical integration, as incentive for
foreign investment, 27–30, 45, 99
Vietnam War, effect on US trade with
France, 74–75
Voluntary export restraints (VERs), 41,
42, 71. *See also* Protectionism

Wages, 145. *See also* Headquarters effect;
Foreign affiliates in the United States
differentials between industries, 57
domestic versus foreign firms, by
industry, 52, 57, 58
in Japanese-owned firms, 61, 64
Wartime, foreign direct investment
during, 73–85. *See also* National
security
Water's-edge unitary tax formula, 106.
See also Taxation
Wholesale trade industry, US
compensation of employees in, 57
foreign share in, 33
misclassification of foreign firms in,
141
Wright, Jim, Jr., 113

Yen-dollar exchange rate, 63–64

Zenith, 40–41

POLICY ANALYSES IN INTERNATIONAL ECONOMICS

1 **The Lending Policies of the International Monetary Fund**
John Williamson/*August 1982*
$8.00   0–88132–000–5   72 pp

2 **"Reciprocity": A New Approach to World Trade Policy?**
William R. Cline/*September 1982*
$8.00   0–88132–001–3   41 pp

3 **Trade Policy in the 1980s**
C. Fred Bergsten and William R. Cline/*November 1982*
(Out of print)   0–88132–002–1   84 pp
Partially reproduced in the book *Trade Policy in the 1980s.*

4 **International Debt and the Stability of the World Economy**
William R. Cline/*September 1983*
$10.00   0–88132–010–2   134 pp

5 **The Exchange Rate System**
John Williamson/*September 1983, 2nd ed. rev. June 1985*
$10.00   0–88132–034–X   61 pp

6 **Economic Sanctions in Support of Foreign Policy Goals**
Gary Clyde Hufbauer and Jeffrey J. Schott/*October 1983*
$10.00   0–88132–014–5   109 pp

7 **A New SDR Allocation?**
John Williamson/*March 1984*
$10.00   0–88132–028–5   61 pp

8 **An International Standard for Monetary Stabilization**
Ronald I. McKinnon/*March 1984*
$10.00   0–88132–018–8   108 pp

9 **The Yen/Dollar Agreement: Liberalizing Japanese Capital Markets**
Jeffrey A. Frankel/*December 1984*
$10.00   0–88132–035–8   86 pp

10 **Bank Lending to Developing Countries: The Policy Alternatives**
C. Fred Bergsten, William R. Cline, and John Williamson/*April 1985*
$12.00   0–88132–032–3   221 pp

11 **Trading for Growth: The Next Round of Trade Negotiations**
Gary Clyde Hufbauer and Jeffrey J. Schott/*September 1985*
$10.00   0–88132–033–1   109 pp

BOOKS

American Trade Politics: System Under Stress
I. M. Destler/*1986*
$30.00 (cloth)	0–88132–058–7	380 pp
$18.00 (paper)	0–88132–057–9	380 pp

The Future of World Trade in Textiles and Apparel
William R. Cline/*1987*
$20.00	0–88132–025–0	344 pp

Capital Flight and Third World Debt
Donald R. Lessard and John Williamson, editors/*1987*
$16.00	0–88132–053–6	270 pp

The Canada–United States Free Trade Agreement: The Global Impact
Jeffrey J. Schott and Murray G. Smith, editors/*1988*
$13.95	0–88132–073–0	211 pp

Managing the Dollar: From the Plaza to the Louvre
Yoichi Funabashi/*1988, 2nd ed. rev. 1989*
$19.95	0–88132–097–8	307 pp

Reforming World Agricultural Trade
Twenty-nine Professionals from Seventeen Countries/*1988*
$3.95	0–88132–088–9	42 pp

World Agricultural Trade: Building a Consensus
William M. Miner and Dale E. Hathaway, editors/*1988*
$16.95	0–88132–071–3	226 pp

Japan in the World Economy
Bela Balassa and Marcus Noland/*1988*
$19.95	0–88132–041–2	306 pp

America in the World Economy: A Strategy for the 1990s
C. Fred Bergsten/*1988*
$29.95 (cloth)	0–88132–089–7	235 pp
$13.95 (paper)	0–88132–082–X	235 pp

United States External Adjustment and the World Economy
William R. Cline/*1989*
$25.00	0–88132–048–X	392 pp

Free Trade Areas and U.S. Trade Policy
Jeffrey J. Schott, editor/*1989*
$19.95	0–88132–094–3	400 pp

Dollar Politics: Exchange Rate Policymaking in the United States
I. M. Destler and C. Randall Henning/*1989*
$11.95	0–88132–079–X	192 pp

Foreign Direct Investment in the United States
Edward M. Graham and Paul R. Krugman/*1989*
$11.95   0–88132–074–9   190 pp

SPECIAL REPORTS

FORTHCOMING

TO ORDER PUBLICATIONS PLEASE WRITE OR CALL US AT:

Institute for International Economics
Publications Department
11 Dupont Circle, NW
Washington, DC 20036
202-328-9000